Dear Todd,

   It has been too long.
Pray you are well. May
this humble work help
you draw a little closer
to our Lord.

                    Peace,

                    J. J. Snell

JESUS HIMSELF DREW NEAR

A SPIRITUALITY FOR SHAPING THE LIVES OF YOUNG PEOPLE

FR. JACK PETERSON, YA

WELLSPRING

North Palm Beach, Florida

wellspring

Design by Kara Ebert

ISBN: 978-1-63582-156-7 (softcover)

10   9   8   7   6   5   4   3   2   1

Printed in the United States of America

TABLE OF CONTENTS

INTRODUCTION

*"These things I have spoken to you,
that my joy may be in you
and your joy may be full."*
(John 15:11)

A few years ago, I was on a weeklong service trip with college students deep in the mountains of the Dominican Republic. The fifteen members of our campus ministry program were just beginning our daily evening program, which was being conducted by flashlight because there was no electricity in the campo (very small village). We were seated outside the town chapel in a circle, some of us on chairs, some on upside-down five-gallon paint buckets, and a few on one small bench. It was quite warm, and we were a bit tired from working in the hot sun for most of the day and then enduring a three-hour ride down a mountain on the backs of mules. We were listening to one of our students give a brief reflection on the theme of serving our neighbor in the name of Christ.

It started off like one of our usual evenings, which were always pretty inspiring. Tonight would be particularly powerful. Gradually, several villagers began to gather around our circle, quite curious about these students from an American university who had invaded their remote town for a week to paint a couple of chapels and build an outhouse. We had been working for two days in two other remote campos and actually had not spent much time yet in this particular little village.

We immediately adjusted our plans, opened up our circle to the locals, and invited them to join our reflection. I asked one of our Latino students, Jorge, to translate for the Dominicans as we reflected upon the example of Jesus' life of service to his neighbor and his command to us to do the same. The young man did an outstanding job. Jorge went back and forth, translating the talk into Spanish and then gathering the thoughts of the locals and translating them into English for our group. He thoroughly enjoyed this spur-of-the-moment task of evangelization. He soon began adding some of his own thoughts to those of his peers as he facilitated a heartwarming and enriching conversation that I will never forget.

At the end of the evening, the wife of *el jefe* (the village leader) said to the whole group in Spanish, "Until today, you have been Americans painting chapels. Tonight, you have become our friends."

I recall with great clarity how Jorge was completely energized that night. His face lit up as he helped two groups of people from very different worlds come together in an animated and inspiring conversation about Jesus and the Christian faith that brought us together from around the globe. We all learned from each other that evening. This young man played a critical role in a very powerful, touching evening program that truly blessed students and Dominican hosts alike.

Jorge had grown up as a Catholic in Central America and came to the United States to earn a college degree in economics.

Before our trip, his faith was an element of his life, but it was not a priority; he was not on fire for Christ. That week, the Lord lit a flame in his heart.

This fire continued to burn as Jorge returned to Marymount University. He describes those early days: "I was shocked at the suddenness and intensity of the change in my life. On the first morning of our return to Marymount, I opened my eyes and I was not the same. I knew a joy in my heart that I had never experienced before. I had a crazy, uncharacteristic desire to do generous things for my peers. I was no longer attracted to certain former, unhealthy attachments in my heart. I experienced God in prayer and at Mass like never before. What I want to say is that God restored my faith, my innocence, and my life almost without me noticing it. It made me think of Mary Magdalene and how Jesus healed her and helped her get rid of bad attachments. God had always been my Father, but after that trip, he was able to make me his son."

Obviously, Jorge's life changed pretty dramatically that week. Like all of us, he experienced bumps along the way, but he began to pray regularly, started going to Mass during the week, joined a weekly Bible study, and became quite involved in campus ministry. Today, he is a dedicated husband and father and a committed Catholic, using his college education to serve the poor in developing countries.

Is there anything more important in this world than helping young people encounter Jesus Christ and discover the joy of being a missionary disciple?

Jorge had not planned to come on this service trip. He was a last-minute add-on because someone else dropped out two days before we left. I was so happy to see his name on the list. We had played some basketball together in the auxiliary gym at Marymount in the weeks before spring break. This gave us a helpful connection that God was able to use. In fact, later in the week, we grabbed one of the seminarians with us on the trip and played two three-on-three games against a team of Dominicans: Americans 2, Dominicans 0.

At the start of this Alternative Spring Break trip, Jorge and I had a wonderful conversation standing on the back of a flatbed truck during the two-and-a-half-hour drive to this remote village. We were enjoying the fascinating, brand-new scenery, dodging branches (and occasionally getting hit by them), tossing candy to children as we drove past a few small Haitian towns that bordered the DR, and catching up about his life before Marymount. It was a casual but meaningful conversation.

When Jesus said, "Let the children come to me and do not hinder them," he gave a mandate to the Church. The evangelization of children and young people is a pastoral priority of the Church and her mission of building God's kingdom on this earth. Young people are a great treasure, a precious gift to be welcomed, cherished, loved, nurtured, guided, and fed with the Good News of Jesus Christ.

As adults invited by Christ to serve young people, we are called to draw near to them, welcome them, engage them in conversation, enter into their lives, accompany them, and introduce them to Christ or help them fall more deeply in love with him.

Pope Francis is rather fond of the notion of accompaniment. We are called by Christ to accompany young people on their journey through the tumultuous years of adolescence in order to bring them the love of Christ. I have found that the process of capturing their hearts for Christ can happen in a wide variety of ways along this whole process. These ways include but, of course, are not limited to a powerful moment of prayer, insight from a talk or homily, a deep conversation about something important in their lives that helps them discover a new insight into the greatness of God, an instance while serving the poor in which they suddenly see the face of Christ, or an opportunity to use a gift while assisting their neighbor that sets their hearts on fire for serving in the name of Christ.

> *"Young people need to have their freedom respected,*
> *yet they also need to be accompanied."*
> —Pope Francis, *Christus vivit*, 242

This book is written for those called to reach out and actively touch the lives of young people with Jesus' sacrificial love and to accompany them on their journey of faith. It is principally an invitation to turn first to Jesus and become a close disciple of the Lord.

If we wish to help young people fall in love with Jesus, we have to fall in love with him first. Young people can spot a fake very quickly. If we are not true disciples of Jesus, they will not be interested in what we have to share with them about the Good Shepherd. So we have to spend a great deal of time in his presence, sitting at his feet, repenting of our sins, being healed by his merciful love, learning the Gospel way of life, growing in virtue, and learning to love with his love.

My experience has taught me that the person of Jesus is enormously attractive to young people when presented properly to them. His unfathomable love is a deep treasure to be experienced, cherished, and explored. His mercy heals the deepest wounds and gives life in abundance. Jesus speaks truths that we need to hear because we are helplessly incomplete without them. He alone addresses the deepest longings of the human heart. Those called by Jesus to bring his light to young people need to find creative ways to get our precious Lord before them, but it all begins by drinking first from the endless well that is Jesus Christ.

The title for this book comes from the evangelist Luke's beautiful story about Jesus' encounter with the disciples on the road to Emmaus. It is clear from his disciples' description of the recent events surrounding the end of Jesus' earthly life that they were dejected and without hope. This state of deep frustration is common among young people.

Jesus teaches us so much about evangelization with the simple fact that he "drew near" to his followers. He sought them out and drew near to these wounded friends. He joined them on their journey, entered into their lives, brought new life to them, and gradually revealed the bright light of his truth to them.

This element of Jesus' approach to the disciples on the road to Emmaus is absolutely critical to the Church's outreach to young people today. Outreach and evangelization have to be relational. That is, we have to draw near to the young, spend time with them, enter into their lives, understand their hurts, and gradually lead them to the truth that will set them free, to Christ himself.

With this foundational principle in mind, the plan for this book is fourfold. First, we will look at Jesus' own commitment to young people in the Gospels. Second, we will highlight that

Jesus taught us by word and example to be grounded in a life of deep prayer. Third, we will present critical elements to an effective prayer life, including a glance at Mary as the perfect model of prayer and charity and a look at key aspects of Ignatian spirituality. Finally, we will point out some of the rich signs of a life transformed by the amazing love of Christ that make evangelization effective in today's world.

> *"Being a Christian is not the result of an ethical choice*
> *or a lofty idea, but the encounter with an event, a person,*
> *which gives life a new horizon and a decisive direction."*
> —Pope Benedict XVI, *Deus caritas est*, 1

CHAPTER 1

JESUS AND CHILDREN

*"Jesus Christ made himself little
with the little ones and bore our
weaknesses. He is our master in the
matter of the friendly approach."*
—St. John Bosco, Letter from Rome, 1884

You might be startled by the number of encounters Jesus has with children and young people in the Gospels as well as the number of times he refers to children in his preaching. We learn a great deal about Jesus and the new life he offers to his followers from these events and references. Children are a rich dimension of the Good News. They claim a very special place in Jesus' sacred heart. While this is not the place for an exhaustive review, I would like to take a look at several of them.

"SHE GAVE BIRTH TO HER FIRSTBORN SON . . ." (LUKE 2:7)

Our Lord's own birth in Bethlehem is an appropriate place to begin this reflection. God's Son, the Second Person of the Holy

Trinity, leaping down from heaven and entering this world through Mary's womb is an absolutely magnificent gift of God. His three-year public ministry as well as his passion, death, and resurrection were made possible by this initial act of supreme humility. For those with faith, the mere thought of the Word made flesh drops us to our knees and makes us sing the praises of God from the depths of our hearts. God's love for his dear children who are hurting and shackled in slavery to sin is so enormous that the infinite, all-holy, all-powerful Lord chose to draw near. It is the descent of love. He refused to leave us alone.

The birth of Jesus in a stable proclaims that God is approachable. I remember vividly the day my older sister gave birth to her first son, Bobby. When I made it to the hospital, my first response was to press my nephew close to my heart, give him a hug, and kiss him on the cheek. Infants, by their very nature, invite us to draw near. God draws near to us so that we can draw near to him. Jesus continues to draw near to us throughout his earthly journey and indeed for all eternity.

The incarnation of Jesus also speaks directly to young people. It informs them that God understands what it means to be a young person. He understands not by squinting from a distance or by gathering and analyzing data, but through personal experience. Jesus fully grasps the needs and challenges that young people face each day. This element of our faith can be a source of comfort to them.

Additionally, the nativity of our Lord proclaims that God dove fully into our human condition and experienced all that we experience, except sin. In particular, Jesus did not skip out on the difficult parts of our human nature. He knows what it is like to get a splinter, go hungry, become a refugee, have a friend die, and be rejected by his peers. He did not even skip adolescence. Jesus dove into all the difficult dimensions of our lives to make clear his great love for us, to bless these difficult dimensions and transform them into channels of his grace.

Furthermore, the birth and childhood of Jesus were marked by a simplicity of life and a humility that are a strong, loving challenge to young people in the world today. Jesus taught by the example of his simplicity of life the need to keep our focus on God and family, on what is truly important in life. It is far too easy to get distracted by the pursuit of material things and lose sight of what leads to genuine fulfillment. Jesus was born in a stable, not a modern hospital; he grew up in the tiny town of Nazareth, not Washington, D.C.; he was the son of a carpenter, not a prime minister. God himself chose the way of humility and simplicity. This is something that young people need to ponder in prayer today.

"AND WHEN HE WAS TWELVE YEARS OLD . . ."
(LUKE 2:41–52)

One could argue that the finding of Jesus in the Temple was one of the most difficult moments in the life of Mary and Joseph, not just in their parenting lives but in the whole of their lives. This is true not because they were panic-stricken while searching for our Lord for three days, which was indeed a cause of enormous anxiety, but because of what our young Savior said to them once he was found. After the great relief of laying eyes on their missing son, Mary understandably confronts her twelve-year-old with the words, "Son, why have you treated us so? Behold, your father and I have been looking for you anxiously." Jesus responds in a way that leaves them puzzled: "How is it that you sought me? Did you not know that I must be in my Father's house?"

The Word made flesh, who could not have been any more obedient to Mary and Joseph, now had a lesson for them. Jesus is first and foremost the Son of his heavenly Father. The principal commitment of his very existence is to the will of his heavenly Father. The Father and the Son had a mission for Jesus' life on this earth that Mary and Joseph would not always grasp. As holy as they were, their perspective on God's plan was limited. Therefore, even Mary, whose outlook on life was not tainted like ours with the darkness of sin, had much to learn from God. None of us can govern God or fit him into our own, limited perspective. His wisdom is beyond human wisdom. "'For my thoughts are not your thoughts, neither are your ways my ways,' says the Lord. 'For as the heavens are higher than the earth, so are my ways higher than your ways and my thoughts than your thoughts'" (Isaiah 55:8–9). This moment remains a lesson for us all. We must strive with all our being to hear and do the will of the Father.

Another angle to point out from this significant event in the early life of Christ is that the young are capable of deep faith and holiness. Mary and Joseph learned a lesson from their twelve-year-old son that day. God has a history and pattern of calling young people to heroic deeds and beautiful heights of faith. King David and the prophet Jeremiah stand out in the Old Testament. The Virgin Mary and John the Evangelist stand out in the New Testament. And for the past two thousand years, how many young saints has God raised up in the Church? St. Agnes, St. Christina, and St. Aloysius Gonzaga sit on that mantel. Closer to our own day, St. Dominic Savio, St. Maria Goretti, Blessed Pier Giorgio Frassati, and Blessed Chiara Luce Badano have joined them. If you are looking for inspiration for yourself or your young people, look up these saints on your favorite search engine.

Our Western culture today is losing its direct connection with our Christian roots and morals. The result is a wearisome battle with an increasingly confused and at times pagan culture. That reality, coupled with a gradual lessening of the practice of the Christian faith in many households, has led a growing number of adults to give up on young people. As a result, many adults feel less capable of inviting young people to live the faith authentically and to embrace the high moral standards that are presented in the Gospels, especially with regard to proper use of the gift of human sexuality. Many adults have given up the battle and are sadly letting the modern culture form the consciences of their children. This is a great tragedy!

Jesus and the Church loudly scream *no* to this trend. Young people are very capable of drawing close to Jesus, engaging a strong prayer life rooted in the Scriptures and the sacraments, building Christian community with their families and peers, and generously serving their neighbors in need. We must remain committed to the fight to prevent various forces in our culture from stealing from us the firm conviction that God wants his little ones close by his side and that he expects their faith to be strong.

"LET THE CHILDREN COME TO ME . . ."
(MARK 10:14)

Jesus' disciples, in keeping with the religious and social customs of the day, tried to push the children away from our Lord as they were gathering close to him. Young people (and women) did not spend time in public with rabbis. Jesus forwent these customs, drew the children close, and engaged them publicly for all to see. He boldly stated, "Let the children come to me; do not hinder them" (Mark 10:14). One senses a measure of considerable frustration with his disciples, because children were an absolute priority to Jesus and his ministry. They must be a high priority for the Church as well. "For to such belongs the kingdom of God" (Mark 10:14).

Jesus extends to young people time, attention, and touch. Young people almost always appreciate it when someone in authority takes the time to give them personal attention that is not focused on chastising them. I will forever recall a moment in high school when an Immaculate Heart of Mary (IHM) sister, Sr. Arlene McCann (who used the name Sr. Robert Therese in those days), asked to jump into the batting cage during my baseball practice and hit a few pitches. She stepped into the cage on a cool spring afternoon with a measure of confidence and tossed her blue scapular over her shoulder. I began to lob a few baseballs, which she hit well. I threw a few pitches a little harder and she hit them as well. I was captivated. Her interest in my world was very touching. It naturally invited me to pay more attention to her world of faith in Jesus, prayer, and service. That unforgettable effort to reach out and actively enter my world did more for my faith in Jesus than a whole semester of religion classes.

"We must have as our primary aim the care of youth, and any occupation that distracts us from this is not good."
—St. John Bosco, *Biographical Memoirs* 14, Chapter 11

Another dimension of this beautiful moment in the Gospels is that twice in this brief passage, the evangelist Luke refers to Jesus touching the children. In addition to showing his care by giving them his precious time and focused attention, Jesus wanted them to physically feel his care: "And he took them in his arms and blessed them, laying his hands on them" (Mark 10:16). We have all known the blessing of an adult whose selfless, caring, appropriate touch at a certain moment brought healing and encouragement.

The use of physical touch in ministry to young people is a highly sensitive topic because of the amount of abuse that so many of them have tragically suffered at the hands of priests and others who have served in the name of the Church, the state, or sports. Any instance of physical, emotional, or sexual abuse is completely intolerable; it is one of the gravest offenses. We who are committed to bringing young people to Christ must do everything within our power to make sure that they are treated with utmost respect and appreciated as the dearest treasures of the Church. They are precious to the Lord and demand the kind of healthy and holy care that is fitting to such treasures.

"You cannot have affection without this familiarity, and where affection is not evident, there can be no confidence. If you want to be loved, you must make it clear that you love."
—St. John Bosco, Letter from Rome, 1884

The Church is rightly demanding that those who work with youth be extra prudent, given our past and given how vulnerable and sensitive young people are. The Church is demanding that those serving them have a solid understanding of their own sexual development and do not engage in ministry unless they are selflessly doing so for the sake of Christ and for the sake of bringing youth to Christ. This means that we do not use young people in any way for personal gain.

Given these most important and legitimate concerns, we cannot deny that Jesus' own example of service to youth included prudent, healthy touch. A hand on the shoulder, a tousling of the hair, or a warm embrace can be a Christlike way to bring God's care to a young person.

"AND HE TOOK A CHILD, AND PUT HIM IN THE MIDST OF THEM . . ." (MARK 9:36)

Our Lord's humility is one of the defining elements of his earthly life. It truly marked every dimension of his life. It was something that greatly influenced the life and spirituality of St. Francis of Assisi. The merchant's son turned poor man had a very strong devotion to Jesus at the three most humble moments of our Lord's earthly journey, each of which were connected to wood: the wood of the crèche, the wood of the cross, and the wood of the altar.

In this Gospel passage, when confronted with the ugly pride of his disciples, Jesus teaches them a lesson about the supreme importance of humility. As they are traveling toward Capernaum, the apostles slip into a pitiful argument about which of them is the greatest. Jesus confronts them about this discussion: "What were you discussing along the way?" They understandably fall silent. So Jesus sits down, assuming the position of a teacher in that culture, and says, "If anyone would be first, he must be last of all and servant of all." Then, our Lord, ever the youth minister, "took a child, and put him in the midst of them; and taking him in his arms, he said to them, 'Whoever receives one such child in my name receives me; and whoever receives me, receives not me but him who sent me'" (Mark 9:33–37).

The sin of pride is at the heart of every sin because it was at the heart of the first sin of Adam and Eve. Our first human parents convinced themselves that they knew better than God what is true and what leads to human fulfillment, and so they ate what was expressly forbidden by the Lord. The sin of pride never stops trying to rear its ugly head in our lives.

Jesus patiently and lovingly transforms this sad turn of events into a teaching moment. This is a powerful example for those who try to serve young people. God is asking us to be patient with our students. He is asking us to recognize their weaknesses, love them in spite of them, and choose the way of patiently inviting them to see the light of Christ and learn from the Lord the path to human flourishing.

Jesus teaches us subtly that one effective way to combat pride and learn humility is to receive and welcome young people in his name. Once again, he is summoning the Church to make the service of young people a pastoral priority in its mission of evangelization.

It is worth noting here that Jesus speaks only of receiving a child in his name. Some translations use the verb *welcome*. For Jesus, the first step in our service to youth is to receive and genuinely welcome them. I recall a Catholic retreat that I attended in college. It was offered to all university students in the state of Virginia. We were about fifty students that weekend. The adult leader had the names of every student memorized in advance and called each of us by name as we entered the retreat center. I was very pleasantly surprised by this gesture. It was a marvelous way to welcome us.

The relational ministry that marks all service in the Church in Christ's name begins with receiving and welcoming. Young people will not normally come to Jesus or to our youth events if they do not feel welcomed. In our work with the young Church, we cannot lead with doctrine and morals. We have to lead with welcoming and friendship. Once friendship and trust are established, then their hearts are open to encounter Christ through us and the opportunities we provide. Once they encounter Christ and are touched by his love and mercy, then they are willing to listen to what he has to say about the Father and about this new way of life presented in the Gospels. They are open to the fascinating and challenging adventure of the disciple of Jesus. It all starts with warmly receiving and welcoming them.

"UNLESS YOU TURN AND BECOME LIKE CHILDREN . . ." (MATTHEW 18:3)

Jesus teaches us that in addition to making young people a pastoral priority of the Church, we should take the time to learn from them. Just as we learn about God from the poor, we learn about him from the young. Our blessed Lord thinks there are ways of being childlike that we should imitate.

Have you taken the time to watch a three- or four-year-old child interact with strangers in the presence of a parent? It is a marvel to behold. The leg of Mom or Dad is the safest place in the world. They hang on for dear life, often circling behind their parent in order to hide from those unknown faces who are looking at them. Such children are convinced that they have absolutely no worries when Mom or Dad is close at hand. Gradually, they cautiously wander a few steps away—and then charge back to home base. Next, they will wander a few steps farther, and then race back again to safety with surprising speed. Then, they will go even farther, this time nearly knocking the parent over upon their return from the fifteen-foot adventure out into the world. For a child, there is nothing to fear when Mom and Dad are in close proximity; children have complete trust that their parents will protect them and defend them against harm.

Jesus is inviting us to have a similar childlike trust in God the Father's love, concern, and protection for each of us. As his beloved brothers and sisters, we are being called by Jesus to radically trust in our heavenly Father. In essence, Jesus says to us, "If only you knew how precious you are to my heavenly Father, you would stop worrying about so many unimportant things. And in the presence of truly dangerous things, you would put your trust in him."

Some years ago, my nephew reminded me of another trait that is characteristic of most young people. I showed up at my sister's house in late October. My nephew discovered that I had not gone trick-or-treating for Halloween. He felt so bad for me that he proceeded to stomp off to his bedroom, grab his pillowcase full of candy, and give half of the candy to me. I was truly touched that evening by his generosity. Kids often surprise us with their willingness to share what they have with others. If only we were always so generous!

Children in most homes receive countless blessings from their parents, including affection, inheritance rights, food, shelter, and an education. They naturally accept the fact that they depend upon their mother and father for everything good in their lives. While many young people could be better at expressing gratitude to their parents, they understand that they rely upon Mom and Dad for the necessities of life. Jesus wants us to live with a more profound awareness of our radical dependence on him. He bestows immeasurable gifts upon us; for instance, our gifts and talents, our friends, the sacraments, the sacred Scriptures, and the Church. These spiritual gifts need to be nurtured by us, through gratitude, through using them to serve our neighbor, and by living in a dynamic relationship with our Father in heaven.

Children also have a built-in resilience to trials. Physically and emotionally, they bounce back from broken bones, scraped knees, and mean cousins. When the support of their parents is strong and consistent, kids move beyond the bumps of life and forge ahead ready to enjoy and embrace whatever life brings next. As children of our heavenly Father, we can learn from this. When aware in our gut of the Father's personal and immeasurable love, we are able to let go of the past, forget our hurts, and approach each day with joy and hope, knowing that the Father is near at hand.

Young people have a strong distaste for injustice and hypocrisy. When adults treat one group of people much differently than another, or when they say one thing and do another, it stirs up in kids' hearts frustration and anger. They innately recognize that people need to be treated fairly and justly. Plus, they can often pick out a phony adult in a matter of moments. Young people call us to treat all God's children with fairness and respect and to live in radical truth.

Often, children have an endearing innocence about them. Especially when the support from their parents is strong, they go through life doing what it sets before them and do not spend much time worrying about tomorrow. They wear the clothes they want that day, they are fine without a shower, and they hang out with whomever they like at school, regardless of race or religion. As children of God, we can learn to spend much less time worrying about what others think of us and be free to live our lives each day as God wants us to. We can grow in our ability to let go of the fact that some may dislike us because we are Christian, have high moral standards, or make sacrificial decisions for the sake of our belief in Christ.

The last childlike quality that I would like to address is a contagious enthusiasm for life. Children are always ready to play a fun game, laugh at a decent joke, take a break for a friend, jump in a puddle, or listen to a favorite song. We adults need to stop taking ourselves so seriously, focusing too much on the problems in our lives, and failing to taste and enjoy God's countless blessings. We need to be able to enjoy precious moments with God, family, and friends that re-create us and renew the soul. We need to spend more time marveling at the wonders of God and recounting them to others.

This is, perhaps, a good place to say a word about young people who have grown up in difficult homes. Not all have completely positive experiences with their parents in the home. Some have even been significantly wounded by parents who are themselves hurting deep inside and are unable to give proper and consistent care to their children. These wounds can be deep and can, in turn, make it difficult to experience God as a loving parent who cares for us beyond our wildest imagination.

This is a very unfortunate situation that significantly disrupts the healthy emotional and spiritual development of a young person. It demands additional patience, wisdom, and care on the part of those entrusted with welcoming them and forming them in the faith.

Ultimately, our Christian faith is an invitation to those from difficult family backgrounds to grow in their awareness and acceptance of the truth that our heavenly Father is the source and perfection of all fatherhood and motherhood. One of Jesus' main tasks during his earthly ministry was to reveal to us the face of God, our Father. He revealed a Father filled with compassion (parable of the Good Samaritan), mercy (parable of the Prodigal Son), goodness (resurrection of Jesus), second chances (call of St. Matthew), and truth (blessed are the poor in spirit). We are invited to experience all this goodness and to trust that we are recipients of his amazing love. We are invited to set aside, over time and with much grace, prayer, and assistance from others, our broken notions of parenting and to learn to trust our heavenly Father.

This process of growing in our trust of our heavenly Father can be long and complicated, but it's a most worthwhile adventure. A solid Catholic or Christian psychologist or counselor can be a major support along the way. Most pastors are familiar with good local ones. A skilled and prayerful spiritual director can be a huge help as well.

"AND JESUS, LOOKING UPON HIM, LOVED HIM . . ." (MARK 10:21)

The story of the rich young man is another wonderful example of a Gospel encounter with Christ. Jesus always engages people on a personal level. He discovers (well, he actually already knows!) what is going on in their lives, what is weighing on their hearts, and what their greatest needs are. Then, he demonstrates his love and mercy, eventually revealing his identity to them. In the midst of this, they come to a deeper understanding of themselves as children of God, which leads to a conversion of heart and a resolve to live a brand-new way of life, the Gospel way of life.

The deciding factor in these encounters is the powerful awareness that in spite of their sins, Jesus loves them and considers them precious. In fact, because of their sins, Jesus loves them and wants to pull them out of the downward spiral of sin and selfishness that leads to boredom, depression, and meaninglessness. He wants to forgive them, set them free from slavery to sin, give them new life through the Holy Spirit, and grant them a new mission of building a culture of love and truth.

In this story, the evangelist Mark specifically emphasizes that Jesus makes his love for the young man clear and evident. "And Jesus, looking upon him, loved him . . ." That love drives Jesus to challenge the young man to do something radical. Jesus knows in his infinite wisdom the Father's plan for the curious young man. Since it is the Father's will, accepting this challenge from Jesus is what will bring the greatest joy and meaning to his life. Jesus loves us completely, at each and every moment of our lives, but he loves us too much to leave us there. Our Lord calls to new life in him, life in abundance. And so, he never hesitates to invite us to change our lives and to do great things for the glory of God.

We must not be afraid to extend the challenge of the Gospel way of life to the young people entrusted to our care. This challenge needs to be done in a similar context. We must first engage the students where they are in life. Then we build a relationship of trust based upon genuine care, openness, and truth. Then we invite them to encounter Christ and his merciful love, or to engage him on a deeper level. Finally, we commit to journeying with them through their formative years, assisting and encouraging them during the difficult times that mark a young person's life.

We know that in this instance, the young man refused Jesus' love and turned down the challenge. It is a stark reminder that it is very difficult for young people to both accept Jesus' offer of mercy and love and respond to him by turning their lives over to him. Service to young people in the Church can be very disheartening at times. We can easily be tempted to give up this form of service. The example of Jesus is an invitation to his apostles to youth to persevere in the task of pre-evangelization, always striving to find creative ways to encourage openness to a genuine encounter with Jesus Christ. It is a call to give until we have no more to offer.

The young man's rejection did not keep Jesus from extending the challenge. Without a doubt, it was a very sad moment for our Lord. But it is likely that the seeds Jesus planted during this encounter took root deep within the youth's heart. I am of the opinion that after a time of pondering this momentous encounter with God's Son, the young man later became a disciple of the Lord. The gaze of love pierced his heart, and in the end, the thrill of being commissioned to do something spectacular for God and neighbor melted his selfishness. He came back to Jesus, fell to his knees, and said in imitation of Peter, "To whom shall I go? You have the words of eternal life."

"LITTLE GIRL, I SAY TO YOU, ARISE."
(MARK 5:41)

We turn next to a scene following the crossing of the Sea of Galilee. Jairus, an official in the Jewish synagogue, approaches Jesus in tremendous pain, but with enough faith in God to have a glimmer of hope. His daughter is sick and dying, and he pleads with Jesus to come to his home and heal her. Jesus graciously agrees but is delayed on the journey by the needs of a woman with a twelve-year-long battle with bleeding. While Jesus is extending a healing touch to this woman, Jairus' daughter dies. Word of this terrifying news is brought to Jairus. He offers to let Jesus go on to other concerns; however, the Lord has another plan. Jesus goes to the house anyway. He tells the mourners who have gathered according to custom to stop their wailing, grabs Peter, James, John, and Jairus and his wife, and approaches the girl's bed. Then, in a gesture that begs prayerful reflection, Jesus takes her by the hand and says to her, "Little girl, I say to you, arise."

One can only imagine the joy and exultation in the hearts of Jairus and his wife. One can only imagine the spring in the step of this twelve-year-old child, who gets up and begins to walk around the house. One can only imagine the surprise on the faces of Peter, James, and John as they witness the raising of a dead child.

May we who journey with God's little ones have a burning desire to bring Christ to young people so that he may take them by the hand and bring them newness of life.

Some years ago, a young woman responded to God's grace and worked up the courage to share with me that she had been abused as a child by an adult in her life. She carried with her for several years a certain guilt that she had somehow been partly responsible for his actions. This misguided sense of responsibility weighed very heavy on her heart. She also admitted that she had not wanted to tell anyone, including me, because she'd thought that I would think less of her. When I patiently listened to her story, extended care to her, made it clear that I respected her greatly for having the courage to share this dark secret, and strongly stated that she had no responsibility for this adult's actions in her life, it was a life-changing moment for her. It was a kind of rising from the dead. Her countenance changed radically that day. The joy and light that radiated from her face was extraordinary. She received the sacraments with such fervor that weekend, diving into her faith with zeal and consistency. She remains a strong Catholic to this day.

> *"We were buried, therefore, with him by baptism into death,*
> *so that as Christ was raised from the dead by the glory*
> *of the Father, we too might walk in newness of life."*
>
> (Romans 6:4)

"DAUGHTERS OF JERUSALEM, DO NOT WEEP FOR ME, BUT FOR YOURSELVES AND FOR YOUR CHILDREN." [LUKE 23:28]

For our final reflection, we turn to the end of Jesus' earthly journey. He finds himself on the way to the cross and is enduring the most difficult time of his earthly existence. He has just been betrayed by Judas in the Upper Room, abandoned by the apostles in the garden, denied by Peter in the courtyard, falsely accused by the Sanhedrin, and scourged by Roman soldiers at the pillar. In this moment, our precious Lord is carrying his cross to Golgotha. What burdens his heart the heaviest is, of course, the immeasurable weight of the whole world's sins. Yet Jesus is so filled with divine charity and compassion that he is able to set aside his suffering and pour out his love on the flock once again. He pleads with the women to shed tears not for him but for themselves and their children.

Once again, Jesus expresses his concern for children. This moment is unique because our Lord is completely immersed in his darkest hour. Yet in spite of an agony that we will never fully comprehend, he invites the world and the Church to be mindful of her young people—to have compassion for them and their sufferings. Our blessed Lord's example of generous and focused concern for children continues to the very end.

> *"Every young person who feels called to a mission*
> *in this world is invited to hear the Father speaking*
> *those same words within his or her ear:*
> *"You are my beloved child."*
> —Pope Francis, *Christus vivit*, 25

CHAPTER 2

JESUS AND PRAYER

*"Prayer in my opinion is nothing else
than the intimate sharing between friends;
it means taking time frequently to be alone
with him who loves us."*
—St. Teresa of Ávila

Jesus, the consummate teacher, was a master of using simple, everyday images to help his followers better understand the central mysteries of our Christian faith, one of which is how the Lord wants very much to be united with us in an intimate relationship of love, knowledge, and service. To explain this mystery, he turned to the everyday image of the vine and the branches: "I am the vine, you are the branches. He who abides in me, and I in him, he it is that bears much fruit, for apart from me you can do nothing" (John 15:5).

It is not hard to grasp how critical it is for a branch to remain connected to the vine in order to live and bear fruit. I recently visited a vineyard in Italy at the beginning of the harvest season. One image from that visit remains imprinted upon my memory: Right next to a row of healthy vines with lush, green leaves and plump, juicy grapes was a pile of branches, brown, shriveled up, and ready for the fire. The contrast was rather stark. The branch that remains united to the vine stays green and healthy and bears much fruit. The branch that gets separated dries up, dies, and is placed in the fire. Jesus chose to emphasize the absolute necessity of this connection: "For apart from me, you can do nothing."

If we desire to maintain our new life in Christ, we must remain intimately connected to him. If we hope to bear fruit for the kingdom of God, to help young people come to know and love Jesus, we have to stay connected to the vine.

JESUS' OWN EXAMPLE

Jesus taught us about prayer principally through the example of his own life of prayer. First of all, he went off to pray frequently. The Gospels recount that Jesus turned to his Father in prayer constantly, going up on the mountain, retreating into a garden, remaining on the shore of the sea, or joining others in the synagogue. It is clear that he worked his complicated schedule in order to carve out time for prayer: He got up early, stayed late into the night, or left his disciples in the middle of the afternoon to pray. Often, Jesus went off alone for personal prayer. But at other times he prayed in common, bringing groups of his disciples with him. He prayed intensely before all the big events in his life. For instance, our Lord spent the whole night in prayer before choosing his twelve apostles and before the events of his passion. Prayer was so important to Jesus, and it had such an effect on his human nature, that his disciples pleaded with him, "Lord, teach us to pray . . ." (Luke 11:1).

The picture is quite clear: Prayer was not a part-time job for Jesus or something he did when it was convenient. It was critical to his day and to his earthly journey. Jesus' life is an invitation to us to be men and women of deep, daily prayer.

JESUS PREACHES ABOUT PRAYER

In addition, Jesus taught us about prayer through his ministry of preaching. Here too, one might be surprised by how often he speaks about the significance of prayer in the Gospels.

> *"Against such and all other trials and temptations,*
> *Francis over and over again advised his Brothers*
> *to use three remedies—the first was prayer, the second*
> *was obedience, such that one willingly did another's will,*
> *the third was the evangelical joy in the Lord."*
> —Johannes Jorgensen, *St. Francis of Assisi,* 35

CONTRITION

Jesus understood that the all-important virtue of humility is quick to manifest itself in our prayer and is nourished by it. When we come face-to-face with the living God, his greatness overwhelms us, our strength leaves us, and we fall to our knees. Jesus does not desire that the brightness of his light and the power of his might send us away in fear, but that they invite us to bow our heads, bend our knees, and humbly ask for God's generous mercy.

Our Lord tells a parable in Luke's Gospel (Luke 18:9–14) in

which he contrasts two men who go into the synagogue to pray. The Pharisee's prayer is disgustingly selfish and disheartening: "God, I thank thee that I am not like other men, even like this tax collector. I fast twice a week, I give tithes of all that I get." His attempt at prayer consists of comparing himself to his neighbor and citing his own good deeds. In Jesus' introduction to this parable, he states that the Pharisee "stood and prayed this with himself." Jesus seems to be saying that this was not just a very poor prayer, but not a true prayer at all.

In contrast, our Lord describes the tax collector in this way: "standing far off, [he] would not even lift up his eyes to heaven, but beat his breast, saying, 'God, be merciful to me, a sinner!'" Jesus praises the tax collector's keen awareness of his sins and his humble request for mercy. "I tell you, this man went down to his house justified, rather than the other; for everyone who exalts himself will be humbled, but he who humbles himself will be exalted."

Another Gospel story that addresses a similar response to God comes from the prince of the apostles. St. Peter encounters Jesus early on in his public ministry. This moment takes place after a sermon that Jesus offers to a large crowd on the shore of the sea from Peter's fishing vessel. Jesus, the carpenter rabbi, beckons for Peter to "Put out into the deep and let down your nets for a catch." Peter understandably objects; he already spent the night fishing without catching one single fish. In the end, he obeys. As a consequence, Peter hauls in so many fish that they nearly sink two boats. Recognizing that he is in the presence of God, Peter drops to his knees and says to Jesus, "Depart from me, for I am a sinful man, O Lord" (Luke 5:8). We can't pray well if our prayer is not grounded in a healthy sense of our brokenness and sinfulness coupled with a great trust in the unimaginably generous mercy of our Savior.

SACRIFICE OF THANKSGIVING

"First of all, then, I urge that supplications,
prayers, intercessions and thanksgivings
be made for all men . . ."
(1 Timothy 2:1)

Another foundational element of Christian prayer is thanksgiving. It is impossible to have a strong belief in almighty God and not be consistently moved to profound gratitude for his over-whelming goodness and generosity with us.

The Psalms were fundamental to the daily rhythm of prayer for Jesus and his fellow Jews. They remain so for Jews and Christians alike to this day. This is true in part because the Psalms are filled with beautiful hymns of praise and thanksgiving to almighty God. On Sunday morning Week 1 of the Liturgy of the Hours, we pray: "For your love is better than life, my lips will speak your praise. So I will bless you all my life, in your name I will lift up my hands. My soul shall be filled as with a banquet, my mouth shall praise you with joy" (Psalm 63:3–5). On Sunday morning Week 2, we exalt God with these words: "Praise God in his holy place, praise him in his mighty heavens. Praise him for his powerful deeds, praise his surpassing greatness! . . . Let everything that lives and breathes give praise to the Lord" (Psalm 150). The Psalms, as part of the sacred Scriptures, were inspired by the Holy Spirit and help give voice to hearts that are profoundly aware of the greatness of God. By praying daily with the Psalms, Jesus encourages his disciples regularly to be aware that God is the source of every blessing in this world and to root our prayer in genuine, heartfelt praise of the Father.

The story of the loaves and fishes comes quickly to mind. This great event demonstrates both Jesus' compassion for the hungry flock as well as his commitment to turn regularly to the Father and offer him a sacrifice of thanksgiving. As Jesus is preparing to graciously provide a much-needed meal for a large dinner party, John the Evangelist tells us that he offered up grace before the meal: "then took the loaves, and when he had given thanks, he distributed them to those who were seated" (John 6:11). Jesus knew that it was the Father's will to take care of this exhausted and famished crowd and that it was not right to proceed with the act of service without pausing to thank his Father for the five loaves and two fish provided by a little boy.

The raising of Lazarus is the scene of another prayerful act of thanksgiving in the life of our Lord, which comes with an intriguing little twist. In this instance, the Lord thanks the Father in advance of the pending miracle. Jesus' will is so united with that of the Father that he knows Lazarus' return to earthly life will happen. Before he raises Lazarus from the dead with the words "Lazarus, come out," Jesus says, "Father, I thank thee that thou has heard me" (John 11:41).

Of course, we can't pass over (pun intended) the institution of the Eucharist, a word derived from the Greek word for thanksgiving. We are so familiar with this moment that we might be tempted to do so. There was an element to this evening that is sometimes overlooked. This was the night when Jesus' "hour" had finally come, the hour when he would reveal his truest identity as Lord and Redeemer. Jesus was fully aware that he would suffer death at the hands of his enemies and surrender his life to the Father for the salvation of our sins. The weight of that offering is beyond our comprehension as human beings, and it was most heavy on his heart. He would, in fact, go from this meal to the Garden of Gethsemane, where his anxiety would so impact him that his disciples would hardly recognize him, and his sweat would become drops of blood.

On that night, with all of this weighing on his soul, Jesus pledged his life to the Father and offered an act of thanksgiving that completely changed the world for all eternity. This act is later confirmed by the actual gift of his life on the cross, which redeems the world from sin. In the Upper Room, Jesus "took bread, and when he had given thanks he broke it and gave it to them, saying, 'This is my body which is given for you. Do this in remembrance of me'" (Luke 22:19).

Catholic Christians are privileged to enter into this redeeming event through the Holy Mass every day until the end of time. We are offered the opportunity to remember with faith and gratitude Jesus' saving act of thanksgiving in the Mass. We are also granted the blessing of uniting the sacrifices of our own lives—that is, our crosses as well as our grateful praise—with the one sacrifice of Christ offered on the cross. Jesus unites our sacrifices with his and offers them to the Father. He allows us to participate in a mysterious way in his saving work. St. Paul speaks of this beautiful, humbling, and exciting dimension of our faith in his letter to the Colossians: "Now I rejoice in my sufferings for your sake, and in my flesh I complete what is lacking in Christ's afflictions for the sake of his body, that is, the Church" (Colossians 1:24).

Furthermore, as if these graces of the Eucharist were not enough, Jesus, at his command and with the power of the Holy Spirit working through the grace of Holy Orders and the words of the priest, becomes truly present on the altar in the greatest of all his miracles. Our precious Lord wants to be united with every one of his disciples in an intimate bond of communion. Love desires to be united with the beloved. Jesus makes good on his promise to remain with us until the end of time: "He who eats my flesh and drinks my blood abides in me, and I in him" (John 6:56).

St. Thomas Aquinas, who is both a doctor of the Church and a mystic, describes this mystery with these famous words:

O precious and wonderful banquet that brings us salvation and contains all sweetness! Could anything be of more intrinsic value? Under the old law it was the flesh of calves and goats that was offered, but here Christ himself, the true God, is set before us as our food. What could be more wonderful than this? No other sacrament has greater healing power; through it sins are purged away, virtues are increased, and the soul is enriched with an abundance of every spiritual gift. It is offered in the Church for the living and the dead, so that what was instituted for the salvation of all may be for the benefit of all. Yet, in the end, no one can fully express the sweetness of this sacrament, in which spiritual delight is tasted at its very source, and in which we renew the memory of the surpassing love for us which Christ revealed in his passion. It was to impress the vastness of this love more firmly upon the hearts of the faithful that our Lord instituted this sacrament at the Last Supper.

The prayer of the Christian is built on the pillars of contrition and gratitude. St. John Bosco said the Eucharist and Penance are two wings that carry young people to heaven.

REST FOR THE WEARY

"Remember that you are never alone, Christ is with you on your journey every day of your lives! He has called you and chosen you to live in the freedom of the children of God. Turn to him in prayer and in love. Ask him to grant you the courage and strength to live in this freedom always. Walk with him who is 'the Way, the Truth and the Life'!"
—St. John Paul II,
World Youth Day, Paris, August 23, 1997

Jesus fully understands how difficult life can be for us. To help us grasp this truth in our guts, he came to earth and pitched his tent among us. The Son of God walked in our shoes for thirty-three years, fully embracing our human condition in every dimension except personal sin. His birth in a stable and his baptism by John are two powerful reminders of this great truth of our Christian faith.

The sin of our first parents, Adam and Eve, along with our own personal sins have so damaged our human nature that our lives on this earth are full of heavy burdens. Even after our baptism, many of the effects of original sin remain in our lives: School and work are a constant toil, life in the family demands incredible self-sacrifice, emotional wounds seem to take forever to heal, learning to love God above all things often feels like a burden, and the development of virtue and true charity is a life-long task. In addition, life often throws additional burdens on us that are out of our control, like sickness, the loss of a loved one, getting fired from work . . . you name it. Life is tough!

Jesus, as our Lord and Savior, never promised that the journey through life toward heaven would be easy. He did promise, how-ever, to be with us and to give us his strength: "Come to me, all who labor and are heavy laden, and I will give you rest" (Matthew 11:28).

Hopefully, we all have had a person or two in our lives whose strength, goodness, and deep care for us has a way of calming the craziness of life. Their very presence seems to lift us out of the mire and bring us peace and hope. Just having them walk into the room can change everything, at least for a few wonderful mo-ments.

Jesus promises to play this role in our lives in a way that only he can, as God, in a way that supremely surpasses how any mere mortal can support us. Because he is God, his personal care, unmatched goodness, and unequaled wisdom are an unending source of comfort. Plus, he is available to us every hour of the day. He invented twenty-four-hour care.

I recall one day, some years ago, being rather overwhelmed by my responsibilities as the General Director of my communi-ty. We were facing a few significant challenges that did not have easy solutions. The lack of apparent resolution was sitting heavy on my shoulders that day. When it came time to celebrate Mass, those burdens were a distraction for the first several minutes. However, God began to pour his grace into my heart through the Gospel story of Jesus healing the Gerasene demoniac. This poor man is possessed by an unclean spirit, lives among the tombs, and wrenches apart the chains of those who try to restrain him. The evangelist Mark makes the point that "no one had the strength to subdue him" (Mark 5:4). Jesus enters the scene, engages the man in dialogue, casts out the demons into the swine, and heals this poor soul. God was speaking to me. Then, at the time of Communion, the Lord overwhelmed me with a wonderful sense of his presence and the conviction that he can do what others can't in this world. He is God. He can solve problems and provide strength for the journey that no one else can offer. I left Mass with a great burden removed from my shoulders, a renewed conviction that I was doing the Lord's work and that he would take care of everything according to his will.

Jesus is the most healing, calming, and rejuvenating presence in our lives. We need to be reminded over and over to turn to him in our greatest need. He provides respite and strength every time we turn to him with faith and confidence.

GO TO YOUR ROOM

"In these days [Jesus] went out to the mountain to pray; and all night he continued in prayer to God."
(Luke 6:12)

"But when you pray, go into your room and shut the door and pray to your Father who is in secret; and your Father who sees in secret will reward you" (Matthew 6:6). This teaching of our Lord, read every Ash Wednesday, is a challenge to our pride, a challenge to avoid praying simply for others to see. But as always, this passage invites us to go much deeper.

When Jesus tells us to go to our room and shut the door, he is making the point that we need to dedicate a portion of our day to be alone with him. Jesus requests some one-on-one time with us every day. God wants our prayer to be an opportunity for a personal encounter with the one who loves us more than we can comprehend. He requests, and good prayer requires, that we carve out an intentional piece of our day (five minutes, twenty minutes, one hour) to get away from life's daily distractions and burdens, sit at his feet, and be united with him in prayer. God longs to have this time with us because we are precious to him. We long for that time with him because we are incomplete without him.

"Your room" refers to a place that you have chosen to set aside for the Lord. It may be a corner in a room, a chair in your sitting room, a bench in your garden, or a pew in a church. A regular physical place is immeasurably helpful. This type of consistency is an invaluable aid to regular prayer. However, in the end, the real "room" is a place in our heart that we have given over to the Lord. Once true prayer is cultivated, we can visit this place no matter where we are physically in the world. This room in our heart is a sacred place where we encounter God on a daily basis.

PERSEVERANCE

"Rejoice in your hope, be patient
in tribulation, be constant in prayer."
(Romans 12:12)

I love playing sports. Sports have been one of God's many blessings in my life. I find great joy in spending time with friends, engaging in the thrill of competition, and enjoying the benefits of exercise. I have come to know that one of the most significant differences between poor athletes and good athletes, between amateurs and professionals, is perseverance. Consistent practice, preparation, and play lead to consistent performance at a higher level.

I love being a Catholic Christian even more than I love sports. I have also come to know that growing in my love for God and my love for my neighbor demands perseverance and consistency in my prayer.

Jesus shares a fascinating parable in chapter eighteen of Luke's Gospel about a woman who brings her case before a nasty judge. Jesus describes this judge as a man "who neither feared God nor regarded man" (Luke 18:2). This is not exactly the kind of person I want making big decisions about my life. Anyway, the woman "kept coming to him and saying, 'Vindicate me against my adversary'" (Luke 18:3). This judge refuses for some time. We know not why. But the woman perseveres in her request. Finally, the judge, wearied by her continual appeals, rules in her favor. Jesus concludes the parable: "And will not God vindicate his elect, who cry out to him day and night?" (Luke 18:8).

Jesus is calling us to persevere in prayer. In fact, St. Luke begins this parable with this statement of purpose: "And he told them a parable, to the effect that they ought always to pray and not lose heart" (Luke 18:1).

INTERCESSION

*"The prayer of a righteous man
has great power in its effects."*
(James 5:16)

One of my favorite churches in the Eternal City of Rome is the Church of St. Augustine. I have always been inspired by the long and difficult conversion God worked in Augustine's life through the gift of his divine mercy, the prayers and perseverance of Augustine's mother, Monica, and the intellectual abilities and personal care of the great St. Ambrose. I love the fact that St. Augustine proceeded to use his own extraordinary intellectual gifts and rich spiritual life to serve Christ and help the Church navigate her way through some very tumultuous times, including a drawn-out battle with the Pelagian heresy. It does not hurt the cause for me that this Roman church houses a masterpiece of the famous painter Caravaggio, *Madonna di Loretto.*

However, another major reason for my love of this church is the chapel to the left of the high altar dedicated to St. Monica. St. Augustine's mother is beloved in the Church because of her deep faith in the Lord and her refusal to give up on her son, who spent many years wandering the globe in search of truth among all the latest philosophies and religions, including Manichaeanism. She longed with all her heart for her extremely talented son to discover the beauty and truth of the Christian faith. She shed countless tears, prayed endlessly, and pursued him physically from Africa to Milan in her effort to bring him to Jesus. Once Augustine was in Milan, her great project was assisted by St. Ambrose, one of the Western Fathers of the Church who would eventually welcome St. Augustine into the Church in the sacrament of baptism.

St. Monica's tomb is present in this chapel. There rest the human remains of a woman who stands out through the centuries as a towering example of intercessory prayer. Her faith-filled heart ached with the love of a mother who longed to see her child discover the greatest treasure on earth. In the end, God answered her prayer and Augustine became a Christian, a courageous bishop, and a monumental saint.

With St. Monica in mind, it should not surprise us that Jesus invites us in a variety of contexts to bring our needs and the needs of others to him in intercessory prayer.

Our precious Lord offered his own prayers for Peter at the Last Supper, knowing that the "rock" would falter and need grace to recover: "Simon, Simon, behold, Satan demanded to have you, that he might sift you like wheat, but I have prayed for you that your faith may not fail; and when you have turned again, strengthen your brethren (Luke 22:31–32).

In the Garden of Gethsemane, during Jesus' passion, Peter, James, and John are failing miserably in their response to Jesus' request that they stay awake with him during his darkest hour. As a result, Jesus invites them to pray even harder for strength during their upcoming trials: "So, could you not watch with me one hour? Watch and pray that you may not enter into temptation; the spirit indeed is willing, but the flesh is weak" (Matthew 26:40b –41).

In the Our Father, the perfect prayer, our Lord invites us to make several well-known intercessory invocations, including "thy will be done," "give us this day our daily bread," and "forgive us our trespasses as we forgive those who trespass against us." The Our Father is charged with intercessory prayer.

One Gospel event shines a bright light on the topic at hand. It is Jesus' encounter with Bartimaeus, the blind beggar. Sitting on the side of the road as Jesus passes by, Bartimaeus hears that Jesus of Nazareth is near. He proceeds to cry out, "Jesus, son of David, have mercy on me." This is a pretty honest, humble prayer. Jesus stops along his journey and calls the poor man to his side. Bartimaeus throws off his mantle, springs up from his place, and approaches Jesus. Our Lord, who is rather intelligent and perceptive, asks this blind man, "What do you want me to do for you?" If I were Bartimaeus, I would have been tempted to be sarcastic and perhaps offered a line like "Would you shine my sandals?" or "Could you spare a bone for my blind dog?"

But Bartimaeus simply puts his need out there: "Master, let me receive my sight." Jesus wanted him to state his request humbly. For the master, it is a great blessing to know our true needs. It is a great grace to bring them with trust and faith to the Lord. This is pleasing to God.

PRAY FOR YOUR PERSECUTORS

"And Jesus said, 'Father, forgive them;
for they know not what they do.'
And they cast lots to divide his garments."
(Luke 23:34)

One aspect of our faith in Jesus that helps convince me that Christianity is universally true is the fact that Jesus is remarkably capable of doing two things at once. He fully understands our fallen human condition, with all our weakness and brokenness; at the same time, Jesus, in his compassion for us, refuses to leave us there, so he loves us, forgives us, heals us, grants us wisdom, and bestows upon us newness of life. He raises us out of the darkness of sin and selfishness and calls us to live in his light.

One of the more outstanding weaknesses of our human condition is the lingering frustration, hurt, and anger that can reign in our lives regarding those who have hurt or persecuted us. Jesus is an expert in humanity. He knows we need to forgive those who have hurt us, surrender that anger to him, and live in the freedom of God's children.

To aid us on this journey of healing and newness of life, Jesus commands another form of intercessory prayer. In the Sermon on the Mount he challenges us: "But I say to you, Love your enemies and pray for those who persecute you" (Matthew 5:44).

We all have a person or two in our lives whom we perceive, rightly or wrongly, as a persecutor. They are the ones who because of their personality, attitude, actions, or omissions have made life difficult for us. It might be a boss or coworker who is extraordinarily selfish and makes the office a place of torture. It might be a brother in our community or a member of our small faith group whose perspective is always different from ours and who regularly gets under our skin. Perhaps it is our own child, who is ungrateful, completely disconnected, making poor decisions, and stubbornly refusing to practice the faith. On the other hand, it could be a parent who, out of immaturity or an inordinate commitment to work, neglects us and fails to be a support for us during critical childhood years.

Jesus asks us to pray for those who persecute us. It is encouraging to know that he is admitting the reality that some people do persecute us. Nonetheless, our blessed Lord is calling us to rise above our bruised human inclinations and move toward love and prayer. By challenging us to pray, he wants us to bring this difficult relationship to him and surrender it to his precious blood. He promises, as we have already addressed, to comfort us and refresh us in our weariness. He also promises strength to do the right thing and develop a Christlike attitude toward those people over time. Sometimes the healing from certain wounds is a process that works out over time. He may inspire us to get needed psychological support, given our individual circumstances.

One fascinating result of praying for the person who persecutes us is that it reduces our anger. It is really hard to remain angry with a person for whom we pray on a regular basis. It is one of the many pleasant surprises that flow from the grace of Jesus Christ.

A FEW FURTHER CONSIDERATIONS

LEARN TO PONDER

The capacity to ponder is unique to us as human beings. It is connected to the great gift of being made in God's image and likeness. We have a built-in ability to perceive and appreciate goodness, truth, beauty, and unity. As Christians, we draw ever closer to the fullness of life by pondering God's marvelous works and allowing them to transform our lives. This gift of God is one that we need to cultivate and develop, especially in the context of prayer.

Two people can look at the same scene in nature, the same passage of Scripture, or the same grace of God working in the life of a saint and have enormously different responses. Two people can stand before the Grand Canyon and one yawns while the other ponders the mind-boggling distances, colors, shapes, and years it took to fashion such a marvel. Two people can see a vineyard from the car window and one thinks of a really poor glass of wine that he had two years ago and the other is drawn into a powerful analogy between the vine and grapes and the Lord and his disciples. Two folks see a picture of a poor man dressed in a shabby burlap sack and one thinks how sad while the other sees St. Francis of Assisi, whose radical commitment to the evangelical way of life brought an immense renewal to the Church starting in the twelfth century.

While it is true that the capacity to ponder God's wonders comes more naturally to some people than to others, there is an art to seeing the hand of God so active in the world, which can be learned and developed in time through prayer.

For example, take five minutes each day to ponder some action of God in your life from the day before. Make the effort to find faith-filled authors who are practiced at noticing God's marvelous deeds, and learn from them. When you do take notice of some great act of God or are lifted up by a beautiful truth of our faith, share it with family and friends via email or at the dinner table.

The splendor of God's truth, goodness, and beauty engulfs us all day long. The Christian must learn to see the Lord and his marvelous deeds, allow them to penetrate his heart and soul through prayerful pondering, and permit them to transform his life.

BEFORE THE BLESSED SACRAMENT

"The church, the house of God, is the proper place
for the liturgical prayer of the parish community.
It is also the privileged place for adoration of the real
presence of Christ in the Blessed Sacrament."
(CCC 2691)

While in the seminary, I was encouraged by my spiritual director to pray a holy hour every day and to do so in front of the Blessed Sacrament if possible. In addition, Mount St. Mary's Seminary provided two hours of exposition and adoration of the Blessed Sacrament on Thursday evenings from ten p.m. to midnight. On the first Friday of the month, adoration continued through the night till Mass in the morning. We were encouraged to pick an hour during the night to spend with our Lord.

I found this time before the Blessed Sacrament to be enormously fruitful for me spiritually. I drew so much closer to the Lord while praying regularly in his Eucharistic presence. I worked through a great deal of my vocation discernment on my knees in front of the tabernacle. I dove much deeper into my relationship with the Lord during those days. I also found that my time in front of him almost always led to thinking of various people in my life and gave me a heart to reach out to them, write to them, call them, and pray for them. My growing love for the Lord indeed spilled over into greater charity toward my neighbor.

I regularly thank God for my spiritual director, who encouraged this practice. We have incorporated it into the life of the consecrated members in Youth Apostles. To this day, that hour in the presence of our Eucharistic Lord coupled with the celebration of the Mass remains the bedrock of my life and my day.

Regular (even daily, if possible) visits to the Blessed Sacrament at the local parish or school chapel are a fantastic spiritual practice: Stop by on the way to or from work, head there during the lunch break, corral the kids and bring them with you on the way to the grocery store, or sign up for an hour at the parish, which has twenty-four-hour exposition. The Lord will not disappoint you. He can never be outdone in generosity.

DISCIPLINE IS CRITICAL

*"And in the morning, a great while before day, he rose
and went out to a lonely place, and there he prayed."*
(Mark 1:35)

Jesus expects our faith to be strong, and he wants our hearts to
be on fire for the faith. The story of Peter walking on water high-
lights our Lord's high expectations. Peter gets out of the fishing
boat and starts to walk on the water at Jesus' invitation. He quickly gets distracted, taking his eyes off the Lord and focusing in-
stead on the power of the sea. As a result, he starts to sink and has
to cry out to the carpenter to save him. Even though Peter is the
only one of the twelve who had enough faith to step out onto the
open water, the Lord chastises him, "O man of little faith, why did
you doubt?" (Matthew 14:31).

Jesus expects our faith not only to be strong, but to impact
the world, to bear fruit: "I came to cast fire upon the earth; and
would that it were already kindled!" (Luke 12:49). This challenge
fits well with the one St. John hears from the Lord and recounts
in the book of Revelation to the church of Laodicea: "So, because
you are lukewarm, and neither cold nor hot, I will spew you out
of my mouth" (Revelation 3:16). Jesus wants our hearts to be on
fire with love for him.

In order to grow in our faith and stir it into a burning flame,
we need to develop discipline. This is not surprising; discipline is
critical in every area of life. At work, being a productive, reliable,
honest team player demands discipline. At home, we need discipline to raise children well, keep a clean house, care sacrificially

JESUS HIMSELF DREW NEAR   51

for family members, and pay bills on time. Maintaining a healthy lifestyle requires discipline to exercise regularly, eat properly, and take medications consistently.

So it is with our life of faith in Christ. If we truly desire to be on fire for the Lord, then we will get to Mass even during the week, go to confession at least monthly, pray daily with the Scriptures, avoid occasions of sin, build Christian community with others who share our love for God, and give of our time to serve our neighbor in need. This Gospel way of life requires a great deal of discipline as well as sacrifice. We have to sacrifice other interests, such as TV, video games, social media, and extra sleep, in order to remain on fire for the Lord.

In his first letter to the Corinthians, St. Paul uses a well-known sports reference to address this very topic: "Every athlete exercises self-control in all things. They do it to receive a perishable wreath, but we an imperishable" (1 Corinthians 9:25). It is sad how acceptable it is in our culture for teachers and coaches to demand so much time, attention, and discipline from our young people while few put even a tenth of the focus on those qualities needed to learn to pray, build a small community of faith, develop high moral standards, and serve our neighbor in need.

Over the years, helping people develop the discipline of daily prayer has been one of the most challenging and rewarding dimensions of my service to the Church as youth minister, campus minister, spiritual director, and priest.

I remain convinced that Jesus is inviting all of us who are committed to being apostles to young people to build a routine of prayer that includes these elements: the Angelus or another morning offering, grace at meals, twenty minutes of prayer that includes meditation upon the Scriptures, daily Mass as often as possible, and a daily examen before going to sleep. It is not so difficult to be convinced that such a routine would greatly assist us in building a life-giving relationship with Christ. What is difficult is developing the discipline needed to make it happen.

Most Christians, young and not so young, find it easy to pray when they are in the mood (after an unexpected blessing comes their way), when it is convenient (they have a delay on the subway and there is no cell signal), or when they are with others who are praying (they are not really in the mood, but they are willing). If we pray only in those circumstances, then our prayer will not be deep. Deep prayer requires consistency, nourishment from the Scriptures, a desire to be alone with the beloved, and a quieting of the heart coupled with a capacity to listen. This process requires discipline, and the fruits are extraordinary.

Discipline in prayer is motivated by the conviction that my soul, my spiritual being, needs daily nourishment as desperately as my body needs food and water. So I commit to carving into my day twenty minutes for personal prayer. If we are new to daily prayer, we may need to start with five minutes and build up to twenty.

This time of prayer may certainly include adoration, contrition, thanksgiving, and supplication (or intercession), but it should also include some time praying with the Scriptures (see chapter three). We must learn to listen to God in prayer, and he promises to speak to us through his inspired Word.

Every one of us must find a time of day that works well for this twenty minutes of personal prayer. Earlier in the day is more effective for most people. I strongly encourage people to try to pray before the day gets going. Once we commence with our daily tasks and arrive at school and work, we are very easily distracted; it is hard to break away physically and emotionally from the demands of life. Plus, most days throw curveballs at us that make it even harder to turn off the switch and enter into a time of prayerful recollection.

Praying in the morning demands serious discipline. It often requires getting up earlier, which means going to bed earlier the night before. That effort demands setting firm limits on the time we spend watching TV, checking social media, or playing video games. Consequently, good prayer begins with our bedtime routine the night before.

You may need to experiment with different times and places to find a pattern that works. For instance, maybe you need to pray before your spouse wakes up or after the children leave for school. You may find it easier to pray after a hot cup of coffee or before reading the news. Additionally, you might want to have your own chair in an out-of-the-way place, or to stop at a church on your way to work. Again, it requires discipline to find a routine that is effective at this moment in your life.

Discipline is another virtue that seems to be in short supply in our world today. However, with God all things are possible. "Dear Lord, we no longer want to live for ourselves but for you. Strengthen us through the Eucharist . . ." (Youth Apostles Prayer).

CHAPTER 3

JESUS LOVES TO FEED HIS FLOCK

". . . at the time for the banquet he sent his servant
to say to those who had been invited,
'Come; for all is now ready.'"
—Luke 14:17

One of the many things that I appreciated about my mother, Nancy, was her passion for feeding our family and our guests at the dining room table. She took great pleasure in setting before us a meal that was delicious, nutritious, and beautifully presented. Even in the craziness of life in a home with young children, she did so on a daily basis while I was growing up. As time went on, she remained committed to this task, particularly during the holidays and for birthday celebrations.

As my mother got up in years, she still insisted on having the holiday meals at her home. In spite of ill health, she would often work so hard preparing for the great banquet that when we finally sat down at the table, she was completely worn out and could hardly eat her dinner. She poured herself out preparing a meal and rejoiced to see her beloved husband, children, and grandchildren gathered around a beautifully decorated table, sharing in conversation and delighting in her culinary efforts.

Parents and friends love to gather the gang for a meal, bask in the company of loved ones, enjoy relaxing conversation, and find out what is really going on in the lives of those dear to us. It brings a smile to my face when I ponder how often Jesus fed his followers.

On one occasion, after an intense period of preaching and teaching in the presence of a large crowd of his followers, Jesus said to his disciples, "I have compassion on the crowd, because they have been with me now three days, and have nothing to eat; and I am unwilling to send them away hungry, lest they faint on the way" (Matthew 15:32). This compassion for the flock led him to perform the miracle of the loaves and fishes, which fed four thousand that day.

We see Jesus' gift of hospitality manifest itself as well at the wedding at Cana. There, he is concerned about the poor couple and their parents as they run out of wine during the wedding feast. Perhaps our Lord felt some responsibility because he had dragged some of his disciples with him to the celebration. Jesus chooses that moment, at his mother's prompting, to perform his first public miracle. And of course he does not provide just a decent house wine; in fact, the head waiter says, "But you have kept the good wine until now" (John 2:10).

The gift of hospitality and the desire to feed the flock remains a focus after the Resurrection as well. Our Lord unexpectedly appears to seven of his disciples on the Sea of Tiberius while they are fishing without any success. Jesus assists them with another miraculous catch of fish, and then, as they arrive at the shore, he has fish and bread cooking over a blazing charcoal fire, and he cries out to them, "Come and have breakfast" (John 21:12).

As followers of Christ and students of the Scriptures, we know well that, for Jesus, most realities in the physical world point to deeper, richer realities in the spiritual world. While Jesus genuinely and deeply cared for the physical well-being of his disciples and loved to be at table with them, all these moments in which he demonstrates his desire to feed us point to the Eucharist. Jesus has an infinitely greater desire to nourish the soul, our deepest self.

> *"Jesus said to them, 'I am the bread of life;*
> *he who comes to me shall not hunger,*
> *and he who believes in me shall never thirst.'"*
> (John 6:35)

THE SUPREME GIFT OF THE EUCHARIST

> *"In that little host is the solution to all*
> *the problems of the world."*
> —Saint John Paul II

The evangelist Luke starts his account of the Last Supper with Jesus speaking these words: "I have earnestly desired to eat this Passover with you before I suffer" (Luke 22:15). The Scripture scholars point out for us that the language Jesus uses in this statement is significant. He makes use of a repetition of the word for *desire*. It might be directly translated as "I have desired to desire to eat this meal with you." Jesus' use of this Aramaic phrase in the Gospels is unique to the Last Supper. That is, he uses this phrase nowhere else in the Gospels.

This leads us to understand that Jesus' greatest desire on this earth with reference to his disciples is to share this specific meal with them and to give them an enduring gift that enables him to remain with them in a most real and intimate way for the rest of their earthly lives. Jesus had to go—he had to fulfill the will of the Father and go to the cross—yet he wanted to remain with the ones he loved so dearly. In his infinite wisdom and power, he found a way to do both: He gave us the Eucharist.

The Eucharist is, of course, a meal. It is a privileged moment for our Lord to gather with his beloved brothers and sisters around the table that he has lovingly set before us. It is a moment to rejoice as we tell stories of the Father's great care for us, recount his marvelous deeds, and ponder his infinite wisdom. It is a chance to speak of what is really going on in our lives, especially as we add our prayers to the general intercessions and unite the sacrifices of our lives to those of Jesus during the offertory prayers. Jesus loves to feed his flock and gather with them around the family table.

The Eucharist is also a memorial celebration. In his wisdom, Jesus did not leave it up to us to craft a way to remember his saving work of redemption. He personally fashioned one and left it to us for the centuries: "Do this in remembrance of me" (Luke 22:19). There is no greater way to recall and celebrate all that God the Father has done for us throughout creation history, but more specifically in the passion, death, and resurrection of his only begotten Son, than to be prayerfully present at the Mass.

The Eucharist is a sacrifice as well. Jesus spoke often during his three years of public ministry about surrendering his life for the redemption of the world. At the Last Supper, he pledged his life for us: "And he took bread, and when he had given thanks he broke it and gave it to them, saying, 'This is my body, which is given for you'" (Luke 22:19). This pledge was brought to a perfect completion on the cross, where Jesus, in fact, surrendered his life to the Father in an act of obedient love that redeemed the world. It is the greatest act of love the world has ever known. That one perfect sacrifice of Christ is made present anew on the altar at every Mass celebrated by the Church. Our precious Lord is not sacrificed again and again. Rather, in the paschal mystery, which took place in history some two thousand years ago, Jesus is, according to God's definitive will, sacramentally made present again on the wood of the altar. How precious is that!

In addition, the Eucharist is a privileged act of thanksgiving. As God's beloved children, we have so much for which to be grateful. The Lord fashions each and every one of us in his image and likeness. He washes our sins away in his own blood. He graces us with the privilege of being drawn up into his love and life for all eternity. He holds us in the palm of his hand and blesses us each day with every heartbeat and every breath we take. He blesses us with family and friends. He bestows gifts and charisms upon us to share in his mission of building his kingdom on this earth, especially among his young people. We can't possibly measure or count the depth and quantity of the Father's gifts.

Finally, the Eucharist is presence. True love, above all else, desires union. In marriage, family, friendship, and the fellowship that marks believers, we long be united with one another in ways that are appropriate to those relationships. Jesus' love for his disciples and his consequent desire to be united with us is one of the great reasons for the Eucharist. You can't be united if you are not present to one another. Jesus longs to be intimately united with his disciples, so he crafted a way to do so for the rest of time. In John's famous Bread of Life discourse, our Lord speaks very precisely about this particular element of the Eucharist: "He who eats my flesh and drinks my blood abides in me, and I in him" (John 6:56).

Many, if not most, of the great saints of the Church have spoken eloquently of the Eucharist, have lived heroic lives nourished by it, and have laid down their lives for Christ in it. St. John Bosco was deeply dedicated to the Mass. He worked with Pope Pius X to make it possible for young people to receive Communion at a younger age and to receive it more frequently.

> *"Every day he humbles himself just as he did when he came from his heavenly throne (Wis. 18:15) into the Virgin's womb; every day he comes and lets us see him in abjection, when he descends from the bosom of the Father into the hands of the priest at the altar. He shows himself to us in this sacred bread just as he once appeared to his apostles in real flesh. With their own eyes they saw only his flesh, but they believed that he was God, because they contemplated him with the eyes of the spirit. We, too, with our own eyes, see only bread and wine, but we must see further and firmly believe that this is his most holy Body and Blood, living and true. In this way our Lord remains continually with his followers, as he promised . . ."*
>
> —St. Francis of Assisi, *Admonitions*, I

PENANCE: PREPARING FOR EUCHARIST

"If we say we have not sinned, we make him a liar,
and his word is not in us."
(1 John 1:10)

Because the Eucharist is the source and summit of our Christian life, a healthy desire wells up in our hearts to be properly prepared so that we may fully participate in the Mass, which, of course, includes the reception of Holy Communion. Following initiation into the Church through baptism, sound sacramental preparation for the reception of the Eucharist, and a desire to receive our Lord in Holy Communion, the only real obstacle to this reception is serious, mortal sin.

Jesus instituted the sacrament of penance knowing we are weak and knowing that in spite of the countless graces God pours into our lives, we still fall too easily into sin. He did plenty to lay the foundation for the sacrament of penance during his public life, especially by offering his forgiveness to so many individuals as he traveled from town to town. However, Easter Sunday night witnessed the formal institution of this sacrament. It took place in the Upper Room, where he had instituted the priesthood and the Eucharist just three nights before.

Jesus came and stood before the ten apostles (Judas was dead and Thomas was conspicuously absent), to whom he said, "Peace be with you." They desperately needed this gift because of all they had been through in the previous week, which, in spite of Jesus' various warnings, they were not prepared to endure. The grace of God's peace is a particular fruit of the Resurrection. Jesus' victory over Satan, sin, and death crowned all his words and deeds and became a river of joy and peace for the whole world.

Next, our Lord recommissioned the apostles: "As the Father has sent me, even so I send you" (John 20:21). He extended to them a unique participation in the ministry he had received from his Father, a share in his priestly, prophetic, kingly office. Then, Jesus "breathed on them . . . ," alluding to the moment in the story of creation when God gave life to Adam by breathing into his nostrils. This is the only other time in all of the Scriptures when God breathes on man. Jesus, through the power of the Resurrection, gave new life to these brothers and to the world.

Our precious Lord then said to the ten, "Receive the Holy Spirit. If you forgive the sins of any, they are forgiven; if you retain the sins of any, they are retained" (John 20:22b –23). With these words, Jesus Christ, the unique Savior of the world, included in this great commission the capacity to forgive the sins of the flock in his name and by the authorization of his heavenly Father. It is hard to grasp that God would choose to use wounded men to be instruments of his forgiveness and healing through the sacrament of penance, but this unquestionably was his plan.

We are called by the Lord to make use of this beautiful sacrament given directly to the first bishops of the Church and eventually shared with their collaborators, the priests. This demands that we humbly make the effort to properly form our conscience and examine it well before going to Communion. When we do so and are aware of serious or mortal sin weighing on our souls, we need to approach the sacrament of penance in advance of receiving Holy Communion. The *Catechism of the Catholic Church* is clear on this practice.

Most of the great encounters with Christ in the Gospels include his extension of his forgiveness to members of a hurting flock. The woman caught in the act of adultery, the cripple lowered through the roof of the house, the woman at the well, and Peter after the Resurrection stand out among these moments. The dual task of bringing people to Christ and preparing their hearts to receive his delightful and life-giving mercy is one of the great joys of being a disciple of Jesus and of accompanying young people.

DAILY EXAMEN

Method for Making the General Examen

"First Point. *The first Point is to give thanks to God our Lord for the benefits received.*
Second Point. *The second, to ask grace to know our sins and cast them out.*
Third Point. *The third, to ask account of our soul from the hour that we rose up to the present Examen, hour by hour, or period by period: and first as to thoughts, and then as to words, and then as to acts . . .*
Fourth Point. *The fourth, to ask pardon of God our Lord for the faults.*
Fifth Point. *The fifth, to purpose amendment with His grace.*"
—St. Ignatius of Loyola, Spiritual Exercises, 43

In the Sermon on the Mount, Jesus issues one of his most piercing challenges: "You, therefore, must be perfect, as your heavenly Father is perfect" (Matthew 5:48). On the surface, this reality seems impossible in every sense and therefore is regularly set aside by most Christians. We must be careful not to push aside a Gospel passage because it makes no sense to us or because it seems too difficult. A puzzling passage like this is an invitation to look deeper and to research the wisdom of the Church.

The Scripture scholars assist us greatly with this passage by explaining that the Gospel writer used a tense of the verb "to be" that is not common or simple to translate into English. Jesus is demanding that we "enter into the process of becoming" perfect as our heavenly Father "is" perfect. Put simply, he is teaching us that holiness is a process. Conversion is a lifelong journey. Be committed to that journey!

With this understanding, one might be tempted to ignore the passage for a rather different reason: I am very far from perfect, and it seems like I have made so little progress in the time I have been serious about my faith. So, perhaps unconsciously, I choose not to embrace this dimension of the Gospel.

Perhaps an analogy will be helpful. Jesus is like a good fitness trainer or teacher. Once we have gotten to a certain level of fitness or understanding of a subject matter, they challenge us to make the effort to get to the next level. They constantly invite us to make progress. The Lord wants us to be committed to growth in prayer, charity, and sacrificial service to our neighbor.

Progress in our life of faith requires a good measure of focus and intentionality. One great practice for staying focused and being intentional about our growth in Christ is the use of a daily examen. Many of the great saints, including St. Ignatius of Loyola, have strongly encouraged the use of an examen each morning or evening as a critical part of daily prayer. St. Ignatius, in fact, encouraged his brothers, the Jesuits, to make an examen several times throughout the day.

The examen is a brief examination of conscience that focuses on two main things: (1) a few specific areas of weakness and sin, and (2) a couple of virtues that we are trying to develop or strengthen at this moment on our spiritual journey.

These specific areas of weakness and sin (for example, impatience with family, lust of the eyes, inability to forgive a past hurt), as well as the virtues that we are trying to develop (for example, regular prayer routine, generosity of spirit when interrupted, humility, courage), are best developed as the fruit of a good retreat or a conversation with a good spiritual director.

The examen should always commence with a prayer to the Holy Spirit for guidance as well as a genuine openness to that guidance. The Holy Spirit is a precious gift that the Father loves to bestow upon his children. "If you then, who are evil, know how to give good gifts to your children, how much more will the heavenly Father give the Holy Spirit to those who ask him!" (Luke 11:13). At the Last Supper, Jesus spoke with great love and devotion about the role of the Holy Spirit, emphasizing that he teaches and guides us in wonderful and often mysterious ways: "But the Counselor, the Holy Spirit, whom the Father will send in my name, he will teach you all things, and bring to your remembrance all that I have said to you" (John 14:26). In this light, we should approach the Holy Spirit with confidence. I might add that many find it helpful to invoke the intercession of the Blessed Mother at this time as well.

The examen does not need to take a long time. In fact, by the grace of God and with some practice, we become sensitive to our failings in these areas throughout the day and quickly see our sins as well as our progress when we take a few moments to review the day in the light of God's grace.

Of course, the daily examen should not be unreasonably limited to these more targeted sins and virtues. For example, we may give in to an old sin that has not attacked us in a while, or we may slide into some relatively new sin or poor attitude. Such realities need to be brought before the Lord and confessed where appropriate as well.

Many graces flow from this daily examen. First, we please the Father by living with a humble spirit of genuine sorrow for our sins. Second, we commit ourselves to the process of becoming perfect as our heavenly Father is perfect. Third, we become quicker at noticing the circumstances or triggers that often lead us to sin, and we become more adept at avoiding them or turning to God for the grace to be more Christlike in those situations.

"For the Son of man came to seek and to save the lost."
(Luke 19:10)

THE TABLE OF GOD'S WORD

"We need to help young people to gain confidence
and familiarity with sacred Scripture so it can become
a compass pointing out the path to follow."
—Pope Benedict XVI, *Verbum domini*, 104

One of the greatest challenges of my life as a priest is to preach the Word of God every day at Mass, especially on Sundays. It is a tremendous challenge to dive into the Word of God, comprehend it, penetrate it, and then open it up to his beloved children in a way that is uplifting, relevant, and challenging at the same time. However, the task of preaching the Word has also proven to be one of the greatest blessings of my life. Preaching the sacred Scriptures is a top priority for me and has forced me to learn to pray with them, fall more deeply in love with Christ, who is at the heart of them, and allow the Scriptures to be an integral part of God's grace changing my life.

Let's return to the story of Jesus and his two disciples on the road to Emmaus. Again, in a wonderfully incarnational way, Jesus draws near and joins them as they leave Jerusalem completely crestfallen. The tone in their words reveals that they are totally dejected over the death of the Messiah. Our Lord draws near and quickly enters into their lives by asking a couple of probing questions that stir up an engaging conversation. This engagement in their lives, addressing what is weighing heavy on their hearts, then opens the door for Jesus to have a deep conversation about the faith: "'Was it not necessary that the Christ should suffer these things and enter into his glory?' And beginning with Moses and all the prophets, he interpreted to them in all the Scriptures the things concerning himself" (Luke 24:26–27).

This encounter on the road to Emmaus, along with the rich conversation about the profound marvels of God, leads to a renewal of the disciples' faith in him. Moments after this extended conversation, the disciples recognize Jesus in the breaking of the bread, and he disappears from their sight. As they ponder what has just happened to them, they recall: "Did not our hearts burn within us while he talked to us on the road, while he opened to us the Scriptures?" (Luke 24:32).

My brothers and sisters in Christ, the sacred Scriptures are the inspired Word of God, written under the inspiration of the Holy Spirit, given to us for the nourishment and instruction that is intended to set our hearts on fire for the love of God.

The sacred Scriptures are one of the most wonderful ways that Jesus feeds his disciples, including his apostles to young people. The New Testament and the Gospels, with their capacity for nourishment and instruction, have a definitive pride of place among the Scriptures.

So, we have the all-important task of falling more deeply in love with Jesus as he comes to us in the Scriptures. Consistent, prayerful pondering of the Scriptures will lead to life-changing encounters with him. We have been given the task of becoming disciplined enough to pray with them on a daily basis.

I recall an Emmaus moment of prayer in my own life. I was a priest serving as chaplain at the University of Mary Washington, while also serving as a part-time parochial vicar at St. Matthew's parish in Spotsylvania, Virginia. It occurred one morning during my holy hour, which I regularly spent in front of the Blessed Sacrament at the parish church. That day, I stepped outside and began to stroll around the building while having a prayerful conversation with the Lord. There was no one around the church that morning. Perhaps Christ arranged this reality for me that day. The conversation started with me unloading my frustrations with ministry and life upon the Lord. After listening to me for some time, the Lord inspired me to stop at the side door of the church, sit down, and rest in him. In fact, Jesus invited me in prayer to imitate St. John the apostle at the Last Supper and place my head on his breast.

I obeyed this prayerful invitation. Sitting with my back against the wooden side door of the church, I used my imagination and leaned against the Lord's chest, allowing him to wrap his arms around me. The conversation stopped completely and I simply enjoyed a long moment of intimacy in our Lord's arms.

I lost all sense of time and have no idea how long that moment lasted. Without the use of words, our Lord gave me a deep sense of his true presence, his immeasurable love, and his promise to be Lord of my ministry and my life. He called me to a new level of trust in him. I have never forgotten that prayer experience.

One hesitation I have about sharing this personal experience is the possibility of suggesting that such moments of deep prayer are common for most Christians. This is not common in my life. Now, it is true that a number of the great saints were regularly blessed with occurrences of intense contemplation and even experiences of what is called "the prayer of union." However, these moments are very special graces that come from the hand of God, and they are not common. Having said that, I do believe that God, at least occasionally, desires to have rich encounters with every one of us.

My experience tells me that God intends to richly bless us with regular moments of good, solid inspiration through our daily prayer with the sacred Scriptures. Jesus regularly touches my soul with a wide variety of inspiration, including a deep sorrow for my sins, a heart full of gratitude for blessings, a keen awareness of the pain being suffered by a family member, a brother in community or a young person in ministry, a new level of patience with a persecutor, or a refreshing insight into a mystery of our faith, such as his joy at forgiving us our sins.

So, how do we pray with the Scriptures?

It begins with simply setting the time aside and placing ourselves in God's hands. It will never happen if we do not try. We
do well to turn immediately and ask for the assistance of the Holy
Spirit. Never forget what St. Paul says: "Likewise the Spirit helps
us in our weakness; for we do not know how to pray as we ought,
but the Spirit himself intercedes for us with sighs too deep for
words" (Romans 8:26).

There are a variety of ways to choose a passage for prayer. We
can select one book of Scripture that we want to work through
prayerfully and reflectively. When taking this approach, I usually
suggest starting with a Gospel or one of Paul's letters, such as
those to the Romans, Corinthians, or Philippians. A second way
is to pick a devotional book written by a solid, well-known spiritual author who addresses passages relating to certain themes
of interest, such as the virtues or vocational discernment. In the
end, I am a strong proponent of using the Scriptures that are
given to us by the Church for daily Mass. These readings can
be found in a lectionary, online (for instance, the United States
Conference of Catholic Bishops, www.usccb.org/bible/), or in
daily devotionals, such as *The Word Among Us* and *Magnificat*. I
think there are abundant graces that flow from praying with the
universal Church on a consistent basis. Those same readings are
used for prayer by hundreds of thousands of Christians each day.
It is good to pray with the Church, and to grow with the mind
and the heart of the Church.

Once we choose a passage to focus on and request the guidance of the Paraclete, one simple way to pray with the Scriptures

is to read the short passage attentively a couple of times. If circumstances allow, read it out loud the first time. Often enough, after you read it reflectively a few times, a line or two will stand out from the passage. This can be God's way of beginning to speak to us. Then, sit with that phrase or line, repeat it, and open your heart to its wisdom. Ask God to speak a word directly to your heart through this passage. If you do not hear anything or sense that the Lord is indeed speaking to you, be patient and try again. If you still do not hear anything, move on to another phrase that captured your attention as you read it.

As we pray regularly with God's Word, the Lord may not grant us a deep, moving inspiration every day. We have to be very careful not to try to force his hand in our lives (tell him how to act), especially in prayer. However, I think that when we do pray regularly, especially with the Scriptures, we can count on the Lord over time transforming our hearts with his limitless love, shaping our minds with his glorious truths, and molding our lives with the Gospel way of life.

I learned another way of praying with the Scriptures in high school from my community and its devotion to St. Ignatius of Loyola. I have found this method to be extremely fruitful in my personal prayer life. St. Ignatius particularly encouraged this form of prayer with events in the Gospels. After prayerfully reading over the passage a couple of times to become familiar with the details, engage your imagination and place yourself in the passage. In the quiet of your mind and with the eyes of faith, imagine going back to the actual event or sermon. Jump into the scene either as a bystander watching from a short distance or as one of the characters in the actual passage. For instance, in the story in which four men lower their disabled friend through the roof of the house into the presence of Jesus, you can be someone in the house watching this event, one of the friends doing the lowering, or the disabled person being brought before the Lord.

St. Ignatius encourages the use of all your senses. Slow down and take the time in this form of prayer to envision the setting, mood of the character(s), light, sounds, smells, etc. In particular, pay close attention to Jesus—his actions, words, attitudes, omissions, as well as the touch of his hand or the look in his eyes. This Ignatian form of prayer is a very fruitful way to encounter Jesus in the sacred Scriptures.

> *"The nourishment of the Scriptures . . . enlightens*
> *the mind, strengthens the will and fires the hearts*
> *of men with the love of God."*
> —Pope Benedict XVI, *Verbum domini*, 23

FRIENDSHIP WITH THE SAINTS

As a young priest, I was blessed to go on a pilgrimage to Italy with a group of brothers in Youth Apostles as well as students from the University of Mary Washington in Fredericksburg, Virginia. We spent a week in Italy visiting a variety of fantastic holy places on our way to Paris for World Youth Day with St. John Paul II.

One particularly noteworthy stop for me was the neighborhood of Valdocco in the city of Turin, where St. John Bosco built his first permanent oratory for poor boys and established the motherhouse of the Salesians of Don Bosco.

St. John Bosco is a patron saint of Youth Apostles. He began as a diocesan priest but discovered a powerful call to dedicate his life to the service of young people. He developed the Preventive System, a method of educating young people that proved to be extremely effective at helping them come to know Jesus and decide to live their lives for him. St. John Bosco also founded the Salesians of Don Bosco, a religious community of brothers and priests, to share in his passion and extend this work around the world. Over the years, I have developed a deep connection with St. John Bosco.

We went directly to the gorgeous church the saint built for the Lord and in honor of Our Lady, Help of Christians. I vividly recall that visit. It began by walking up the main aisle with several students, quietly but exultantly explaining the Scripture passages, the saints, and the events in St. John Bosco's life depicted in the paintings along the way, which I was also viewing for the first time. To say that I was thrilled to be there is an understatement.

When the students and I drew close to the front of the basilica, I saw that the tomb of St. John Bosco was below a side altar to the right of the main altar, as is common in many churches in Italy. We went over to the tomb, which had a long wooden kneeler in front of it. I spontaneously knelt there and began to pray. Soon, I was weeping, somewhat uncontrollably. I remained there in prayer for some time. I was completely overcome by a variety of sentiments. First, I knew a warm sense of gratitude to God for giving me this amazing opportunity. Second, I felt a true joy at being where St. John Bosco had lived, ministered, and developed his profoundly effective Preventive System. Third, I had a deep sense of spiritual kinship with St. John Bosco, who so loved young people and devoted every bit of his life to bringing them to Christ and forming them into good citizens.

I tell this story to help highlight that the saints are a fantastic gift of God to us. They are a kind of living gospel for us to see and even experience. Their lives and their work are always immensely important at a particular time in history and in the life of the Church. They love God so completely, surrender their hearts to him so radically, develop truly heroic virtue, and serve others with such generosity.

One could argue that their role in the Church at the time of their earthly journey is reason enough for them to be exalted in the Church. However, they continue to be a tremendous blessing for Christians. They inspire us through the centuries with the example of their lives, the teachings they leave to us, and the great gift of their prayers from heaven in our own day.

I would like to conclude by returning for a moment to this notion of spiritual friendship. From the many saints on the Church's long list of canonized heroes, the Lord grants us the opportunity to enter into a more personal and intimate friendship with at least a few of them. While every one of them can be a model, an inspiration, and an intercessor for us on our journey through the narrow gate, I think we can build a more intimate spiritual friendship with at least a few of them.

Clearly, St. John Bosco is one for me. But I also claim a spiritual kinship with St. Ignatius of Loyola and St. Francis of Assisi. They are the three patron saints of Youth Apostles. But I have several others, like St. John Paul II, St. Maria Goretti, and St. Andre Bessette, each for very different reasons.

There can be a variety of reasons the friendship is sparked:

They are a patron saint of our vocation; our parish is dedicated to one of them; they inspire us with one of their heroic virtues; we seek their intercession during a difficult moment in life; or they inspire a spirituality that resonates with our soul.

A further helpful reality is that the saints hail from every walk of life and every profession. There are kings and slaves; lawyers and farmers; spouses and celibates; doctors and doorkeepers; young and old; virgins and martyrs; and founders and followers. With the grace of God, a little bit of research, and some prayer, you will find a friend or two who is sitting around the table of the heavenly banquet and ready to be a most helpful companion on your journey of faith.

> *"The words of the holy Gospel which tell us that our Divine Saviour came from heaven to earth to gather together all the children of God scattered in different parts of the earth, can be applied literally to the young people of our day. They are the most delicate and precious portion of human society, on which we found our hopes for a happy future . . . This was the mission of the Son of God."*
> —St. John Bosco, Introduction to the *Regulations of the Oratory of St. Francis de Sales*

CHAPTER 4

JESUS GIVES US HIS MOTHER

"Do not be afraid, Mary,
for you have found favor with God."
—Luke 1:30

It is well-known that people tend to make very important gifts to loved ones when they approach the end of their lives. The same is unquestionably true for Jesus. In the last hours of his life and during his final moments alone with the apostles, he gave us (instituted) two awesome sacraments, the priesthood and the Eucharist. Moments before his last breath, Jesus gave us the gift of his mother: "'Woman, behold, your son!' . . . 'Behold your mother'" (John 19:26–27). This gift is one more exquisite example of Jesus' profound desire to bless and nourish us with everything we need along the path of this world to heaven. He wanted to share even his mother with us.

Mary is a precious gem who has consistently captivated the hearts of Christians and artists from the earliest days of Christianity. The number of churches, altars, paintings, frescoes, and statues in Rome dedicated to the honor of our Blessed Mother is truly astounding. It is both a natural and supernatural expression of the supreme blessing that she is to the Church and to the world.

MARY'S RADICAL YES

One moment in Mary's life that properly draws attention is the Annunciation. One of my favorite paintings in Rome of this grace-filled moment is located in a chapel dedicated to Mary, just to the right of the tomb of St. Ignatius of Loyola, in the renowned Jesuit church Chiesa del Gesù. More on that in a moment.

God offers to Mary, with the assistance of the angel Gabriel, the opportunity to be the God bearer and to assume the most significant role possible for a human being in the saving work of his only begotten Son. This event, a critical moment in time, is so filled with mystery, grace, and importance that it deserves all the attention it has received through the centuries in prayer, theology, art, and music.

Almighty God offers to a fourteen-year-old girl from the little town of Nazareth the opportunity to give flesh to the eternal Son of God, to humbly protect, form, and serve him as only a mother can, and to participate in the most unique way in the works he will accomplish to redeem the world from sin and death. In this moment rests the future salvation of the world.

St. Bernard has a homily that grants us a glimpse of the importance of this moment in time.

> *"You have heard, O Virgin, that you will conceive*
> *and bear a son; you have heard that it will not be by*
> *man but by the Holy Spirit. The angel awaits an answer;*
> *it is time for him to return to God who sent him. We too*
> *are waiting, O Lady, for your word of compassion;*
> *the sentence of condemnation weighs heavily upon us.*
>
> *"The price of our salvation is offered to you. We shall be*
> *set free at once if you consent. In the eternal Word of God*
> *we all came to be, and behold, we die. In your brief response*
> *we are to be remade in order to be recalled to life.*
>
> *"Tearful Adam with his sorrowing family begs this of you,*
> *O loving Virgin, in their exile from Paradise. Abraham*
> *begs it, David begs it. All the other holy patriarchs, your*
> *ancestors, ask it of you, as they dwell in the country of*
> *the shadow of death. This is what the whole earth waits for,*
> *prostrate at your feet. It is right in doing so, for on your word*
> *depends comfort for the wretched, ransom for the captive, free-*
> *dom for the condemned, indeed, salvation for all the sons*
> *of Adam, the whole of your race.*

*"Answer quickly, O Virgin. Reply in haste to the angel,
or rather through the angel to the Lord. Answer with
a word, receive the Word of God. Speak your own
word, conceive the divine Word. Breathe a passing
word, embrace the eternal Word.*

*"Why do you delay, why are you afraid? Believe, give
praise, and receive. Let humility be bold, let modesty be
confident. This is no time for virginal simplicity to forget
prudence. In this matter alone, O prudent Virgin, do not
fear to be presumptuous. Though modest silence is pleasing,
dutiful speech is now more necessary. Open your heart
to faith, O blessed Virgin, your lips to praise, your womb
to the Creator. See, the desired of all nations is at your
door, knocking to enter. If he should pass by because of
your delay, in sorrow you would begin to seek him afresh,
the One whom your soul loves. Arise, hasten, open. Arise
in faith, hasten in devotion, open in praise and thanksgiving.
Behold the handmaid of the Lord, she says, be it done to me
according to your word."*

(Hom. 4, 8–9: Opera omnia, Edit. Cisterc. 4 [1966], 53–54)

Mary came to this moment in her life with additional grace. She
had been conceived in her mother's womb without sin. This was
a most special grace, a prevenient grace, given to her in preparation for the potential role she would play as the ark of the new
covenant. It was prevenient because it relied upon the future
death and resurrection of her Son, but it was applied in advance
to her because God exists outside time, is Lord of history, and
chose to grant her this gift as it was necessary for the Incarnation

to take place. In addition to this unique grace, Mary went on to remain intimately close to God and avoid any personal sin before the arrival of the angel Gabriel.

Even though she was assisted by all these graces, the Annunciation clearly shook Mary's very soul. She was human and only fourteen years old. She was endowed, like all of us, with the gift of human freedom and needed to respond to this divine invitation.

The evangelist Luke recounts this event for us and notes that upon hearing the storied greeting from the angel Gabriel ("Hail, O favored one, the Lord is with you!"), Mary "was greatly troubled at the saying, and considered in her mind what sort of greeting this might be" (Luke 1:29). She was clearly not expecting this visit and its consequent invitation; it caught her off guard and greatly troubled her innocent and prayerful soul.

So the angel sought to comfort her and further explain his mission: "Do not be afraid, Mary, for you have found favor with God. And behold, you will conceive in your womb and bear a son, and you shall call him Jesus" (Luke 1:30–31).

It is fair to assume that the words of the angel Gabriel and the accompanying grace of the Lord did bring Mary courage during this encounter; however, she faced a new battle— confusion. From a human perspective, this plan did not make sense to her. She responded, "How shall this be, since I have no husband?" Now, it is true that Mary was married to Joseph, but the practice of marriage in that culture was different from ours. They were not yet sleeping together. Plus, tradition teaches us that Mary had made a private vow to God never to engage in intercourse, even with a future husband. So this request to give birth to a son was most confusing to her.

We know that the angel proceeded to explain that this mysterious reality would be accomplished by the work of the Holy Spirit: "The Holy Spirit will come upon you, and the power of the Most High will overshadow you: therefore the child to be born will be called holy, the Son of God" (Luke 1:35). The young virgin thus wrestled with at least two great challenges that day: fear and confusion.

Let us return to the image of Mary preserved on the chapel wall just feet from the human remains of St. Ignatius. The painting portrays a woman who, we might be tempted to say, faces an additional challenge in that precarious moment: humility. The Mary presented to us in this painting is looking down at the ground, stepping back from the angel, and with her hands seems to be saying, "Who, me?" The whole scene suggests that a deep humility resides in her heart throughout this precious visit.

The virtue of humility may have manifested itself in two different but related ways in Mary's soul, both of which, in the end, led to the right decision. First, true humility would make Mary slow and deliberate to say yes, because she would never think this grace was expected or deserved. She would never have thought herself better than others and therefore somehow more deserving of this extraordinary grace. On the other hand, it was real humility, so it was rooted in truth. Therefore, neither would Mary desire to shrink from the call if she discerned that it was indeed God's will for her life. As it became clear throughout this encounter with God and his messenger that it was the will of God for her to give birth to Jesus, Mary soon knew what her response had to be.

In the end, even at her tender age, Mary prayerfully, freely, and joyfully responded with words that stand as an eternal testament to the world and a model for every Christian who claims to be a disciple of Jesus: "Behold, I am the handmaid of the Lord; let it be to me according to your word" (Luke 1:38).

Mary's radical yes is another example of God being willing to use and fully trust a young person to accomplish an important task in salvation history. In this instance, the task happens to be the most important in the history of the world, aside from those that make up the work of her Son.

Mary, in this moment and throughout her life, remains a model for Christians discerning God's will in their lives. It is an invitation to us to be wholly dedicated to accomplishing the will of the Father in our own lives. This process includes but is not limited to: (1) growing in our true desire to do his will above our own; (2) striving to free ourselves from any attachments that distract us from giving our hearts fully to God; (3) learning the art of prayer, which enables us to slow down, quiet our hearts, and listen to God speak quietly to us; (4) developing the grace to discern the various spirits that tug at us, separating those that come from God from those that do not; and (5) building a life of virtue, which makes it easier for us to do the right thing in various circumstances, including new or difficult ones, with a certain ease and joy.

Mary remains a model Christian for all to imitate, especially apostles to young people.

MODEL OF THE CHRISTIAN LIFE AND MINISTRY

The spread of Christianity demands models of the faith. We all need models in our lives—men, women, and young people who inspire us to draw closer to Christ, teach us how to live our faith very practically by the example of their lives, and inspire us to remain faithful when the road is difficult.

The picture of Mary painted for us in the Gospels is of an extraordinary model of the Christian life. Indeed, Christians have understood from our earliest days that Mary is the perfect example of what it means to be a true disciple of Jesus. In that light, my community prays every day in our Youth Apostle prayer, "Let her example be the basis for our ministry that we may become salt of the earth to bring flavor to your Word and light of the world to guide the youth with your light which shines through us." Let's ponder the example Mary gives us in the Gospels.

1. MARY'S LOVE FOR GOD

We have already discussed in some detail the beauty of Mary's response to God in the Annunciation. She overcame surprise, fear, and confusion en route to her radical yes. There is no doubt that her love for God was an essential element of this generous gift of her life to him and his call for her. Her humility and love for God enabled her to make the leap of faith and lay down her life for him before the angel Gabriel.

Quite soon after the angel departs, Mary heads off to the hill country to visit her cousin Elizabeth, who is with child in her old age. Upon Mary's arrival, Elizabeth sings her praises for her faith and for the blessing of her visit. Mary's immediate response to Elizabeth's most kind words is to deflect the words of praise in the direction of God. Again, her humility and love of God reign so prominently in her heart that she immediately launches into the famous Magnificat: "My soul proclaims the greatness of the Lord. My spirit rejoices in God my Savior . . ."

Mary's love for God continued to grow throughout her life and was greatly enhanced by the birth of Jesus. The connection between a child and its mother that develops over nine months in the womb is precious and irreplaceable. Then, Mary, along with Joseph, had the extraordinary privilege of raising Jesus. Her love for God grew as she nursed him, taught him to pray with the Psalms, bandaged his scrapes, and encouraged his efforts to learn Joseph's trade as a carpenter.

Then, there was the cross. The Gospels make it clear that Mary was there, faithful and true, till the end. The apostles were weak and fickle throughout Jesus' passion, but Mary was a rock. One can easily imagine that her unbroken faith and bountiful love brought comfort to our Lord in his darkest hour. Her presence, her glance, and her loving touch were his greatest earthly comforts in those final hours.

It is safe to say that no one has ever loved Jesus like Mary.

2. MARY'S FAITH

"Wherefore, [Mary] is hailed as pre-eminent and as
a wholly unique member of the Church, and as its type
and outstanding model in faith and charity."
(*Lumen gentium*, 53)

Elizabeth's response to Mary's visit is marked by her own beautiful act of humility. She turns to her younger cousin with the divine infant in her womb and says, "And why is this granted me, that the mother of my Lord should come to me?" (Luke 1:43).

Next, Elizabeth expresses great appreciation for Mary's faith in God: "And blessed is she who believed that there would be a fulfillment of what was spoken to her from the Lord" (Luke 1:45). Oh yes! Blessed is she who believed! Mary conceived Jesus in her heart through faith before she conceived him in her womb. Both conceptions were, of course, the fruit of the grace of the Holy Spirit.

Mary's faith in God the Father and his only begotten son never wavers. Recall the moment during Jesus' public ministry when Mary shows up and tries to make contact with her Son. Jesus responds by saying to the crowd, "Who is my mother, and who are my brothers?" And stretching out his hand toward his disciples, he says, "Here are my mother and my brothers! For whoever does the will of my Father in heaven is my brother, and sister, and mother" (Matthew 12:48–50). Mary is not at all offended by this remark. She is committed with every fiber of her being to doing the will of the Father. She knows that her gift of faith and her zeal for doing the Father's will join her to her Son in a way that far surpasses giving birth to him and nursing him at her breast. It is not that she does not deeply appreciate that sublime privilege, but belief in Jesus coupled with a zeal for the divine plans of the Father who sent him are infinitely greater blessings. They lead to everlasting life.

The wedding at Cana witnesses another manifestation of Mary's remarkable faith. The mother of Jesus is so in tune with the will of the Father that she perseveres in pressing her Son to address the need of the poor couple who are running out of wine. She insists, turning to the waiters and stating, "Do whatever he tells you." We know that Jesus responds to her and proceeds to perform the first of his public miracles that day.

A reflection on Mary can't be concluded without returning to Calvary. It was there that her faith manifested itself most dearly. St. Bernard's oft-read sermon nicely ties together Mary's faith and love at the foot of the cross: "Perhaps someone will say: 'Had she not known before that he would die?' Undoubtedly. 'Did she not expect him to rise again at once?' Surely. 'And still she grieved over her crucified Son?' Intensely. Who are you and what is the source of your wisdom that you are more surprised at the compassion of Mary than at the passion of Mary's Son? For if he could die in body, could she not die with him in spirit? He died in body through a love greater than anyone had known. She died in spirit through a love unlike any other since his" (Liturgy of the Hours, vol. IV, p. 1402).

It is a gross understatement to say that Mary's faith was strong.

3. MARY'S FAITH GIVES WAY TO OBEDIENCE

> *"Rightly, therefore, the Fathers see Mary not merely*
> *as passively engaged by God, but as freely cooperating*
> *in the work of man's salvation through faith and obedience."*
> (LG 56) (Lumegegeniu 56)

Obedience is a dirty word down through the ages and in most cultures. It unquestionably remains so in our present day, especially in Western culture. Our broken and bruised human nature rears its ugly head and manifests itself in a desperate desire to be free of any constraints from man, God, or even right reason to do what we want, when we want, with whomever we want. This path, ironically, leads to the slavery of sin and selfishness. It is a trap cleverly set by the devil himself.

The magnificent truth is that God created us out of love and fashioned our human nature with a marvelous freedom that we might gratefully, generously, freely surrender our hearts and lives to him. When creating man in the depths of his wisdom and love, God refused to make robots that were forced to obey his orders without thought or volition. Rather, he fashioned us to love him, and love demands freedom. We can't love if we are not truly free.

The flip side is that to be truly free, we have to have the capacity to say no to God. This, of course, is the essence of sin—choosing our selfish desires and misinformed will over God's perfect will for us.

One reason that Mary shines so brightly in our world is that she lived a lovingly obedient life. We can say that obedience is the grace of faith applied to situations that are either unclear or just plain hard to follow. Certain aspects of the Christian faith are easier to embrace than others. The birth of Christ in a stable and his profound concern for the poor, the disabled, and the sinners are not too hard to embrace. However, some truths of the faith or the application of them are much harder. For instance, understanding the Holy Spirit as the Third Person of the Blessed Trinity, living celibacy for the sake of the kingdom, and practicing the command to love our enemies all require a deeper response in faith. Sometimes the truths of the faith and the personal requests of God demand an act of faith that feels like pure obedience in the moment. Later we often see the wisdom and love found in these divine requests.

Now this theme is becoming a common one, but Mary bore supreme witness to the obedience of faith at the Annunciation. Even though she was young and lacking experience, Mary of Nazareth chose, in faith and love, to be obedient to God. She had to work through the plan he laid out for her, and perhaps in the end everything was simple and clear, but even if it wasn't, Mary still committed herself to follow God's will.

This obedient faith became a pattern. She followed Joseph to Bethlehem to register for the census and gave birth to Jesus away from her hometown, where she had a familiar environment and family and friends who could have assisted with such a significant event. Soon thereafter, the new parents obeyed the Lord and took Jesus to Egypt to avoid the sinister plans of King Herod.

One of the more challenging moments for Mary was the incident in the Temple. From a human perspective, it does not make sense that Jesus would fail to let his parents know that he was remaining in the Temple for discussions with the experts in the law while the family joined the caravan to head back to Nazareth. Consequently, Mary and Joseph spent three days filled with great angst searching for their twelve-year-old son. Mary confronted Jesus with words that seem reasonable from a human perspective: "Son, why have you treated us so? Behold, your father and I have been looking for you anxiously" (Luke 2:48).

Jesus' response caught Mary and Joseph off guard, to say the least: "How is it that you sought me? Did you not know that I must be in my Father's house?" (Luke 2:49). We are tasting here some of the mystery that surrounds Jesus' life and mission. The Gospel writer says, "And they did not understand this saying which he spoke to them" (v. 50). Our young Savior used this opportunity to teach his parents and the world that his top priority was to remain united to the Father and accomplish his plans. This reality will confront our human wisdom at times and not always make sense to us. It was almost as if Jesus was saying to his parents, "Prepare yourselves for a wide range of surprises down the road as the Father's plan for me unfolds."

Very interestingly, the evangelist Luke then states: "And [Jesus] went down with them and came to Nazareth, and was obedient to them" (Luke 2:51). Jesus was always obedient to his parents, but he was obedient first to his heavenly Father.

Luke finishes this passage by relating to us: "and his mother kept all these things in her heart." Mary wrestled in her heart with the actions and words of her Son and brought them to prayer. She pondered all that happened, remained obedient to God, and worked out the difficulties in prayer. Obedience is not always easy. It demands regular and deep prayer.

4. MARY'S LOVE OF NEIGHBOR

We know part two of the greatest commandment: "The second is this, 'You shall love your neighbor as yourself.' There is no other commandment greater than these" (Mark 12:31). Mary's great faith in God and amazing love for him spilled over into a most generous love of her neighbor. First, let's return to the story of the Visitation to study Mary's art of caring.

It would have been easy for Mary to rationalize staying home after the visit of the angel Gabriel. Her whole life had just been turned upside down and there must have been a desire to get her feet back on the ground. She had just received the new task from God to prepare for the birth of the Christ child. Most women would have already spent some time dreaming of these things and making plans in their head for the birth of their first child; however, Mary had made a promise of celibacy, which God had inspired so that she would be prepared to be the absolutely pure vessel needed to give flesh to the Son of the living God. Consequently, she had given little or no thought to these preparations. So Mary's visit to Elizabeth exemplifies a true selfless attitude that left her free to serve her aging cousin.

It is also significant to note that "Mary arose and went in haste into the hill country . . . and entered the house of Zechari'ah and greeted Elizabeth" (Luke 1:39–40). Our Blessed Mother did not hesitate at all. Mary models for us a charity that is offered with speed. It is so much easier to receive and accept the love and care of another person when it is offered without hesitation. To the contrary, it is so much harder to accept someone's charity when they hem and haw, hesitate, and seem reluctant to offer or do some act of kindness. This approach quickly makes the recipient not want to receive the gift because it seems like it is not given freely and from a generous heart.

Another outstanding element of Mary's visit that shapes her charity is, again, her humility. Some of us, if we were Mary, might have been tempted to think, "I am pregnant with the Son of God; why should I travel all that way to serve Elizabeth, who is pregnant with a mere mortal human being?" I am quite sure that such thoughts never entered Mary's mind. She had such a servant's heart that she went with great joy and enthusiasm to spend time with the mother of John the Baptist. Additionally, Mary did not go there to write a Gospel, begin a new religious community, or erect a basilica. Rather, she went to pray with Elizabeth, do laundry, fetch water from the well, learn to sew diapers, and cook some pasta. Mary went to the hill country with a humble, servant's heart.

My mom would not be happy with me if I did not make the next point. By visiting her cousin, Mary also teaches us the priority of family. My mom reminded me often as a young man that charity begins at home. It is so easy for Christians to focus on and maybe even idealize the charity that we offer to young people, the elderly in nursing homes, or the poor at soup kitchens and neglect to care for those in our own homes as we should. We are tempted to give so much at school or in the office and to certain service projects that we often leave nothing in the tank for our loved ones around the dinner table. Mary, ever in tune with the desires on God's heart, teaches us that charity begins at home.

A final thought regarding the Visitation: While it is true that Mary went in haste to generously serve her cousin with humility,

Mary, in turn, was greatly blessed by the experience.

Picture for a moment her expedition to the hilly town of Ein Karin. Along the way, I can imagine that she prayed for Elizabeth and Zechariah, pondered what sorts of tasks she would offer her pregnant cousin, and began to think about building a home with Joseph that would be appropriate for their Son. However, I do not imagine that Mary expected to be blessed the way she was for those three months. Upon Mary's arrival, Elizabeth received her with humility and deference (Who am I that the mother of my Lord should come to me?), praised her deep faith, and proclaimed that her own son leapt in the womb at Mary's greeting. At the time of her arrival, Mary may have felt a little overwhelmed and alone in her new adventure; however, Elizabeth got it. The two of them must have brought tremendous encouragement to each other. The intensity and beauty of their prayer, conversation, and interaction must have been a great gift back to Mary. This is an integral element of the service we offer to others in the name of Christ. Almost always, we receive much more than we give. It is the way of Christ!

Our next stop on this adventure of learning about charity from Mary is the wedding at Cana. Mary had a radar that was always searching for, aware of, and sensitive to the needs of those around her. There was obviously a healthy turnout of guests at this wedding, yet who noticed the impending embarrassment for the wedding couple and their families? The Christian, in imitation of Jesus and Mary and filled with the grace of God, develops the capacity to look beyond themselves and their personal concerns and to perceive the needs of those God puts in their path. This is a very important element of living and serving in the name of Christ.

Furthermore, it is one very important grace to notice a neighbor's need; it is another equally important grace to do something about it. In this instance, Mary did something concrete: She turned to Jesus for a resolution to the impending need. She reported to her Son, "They have no wine." Mary went to the one who could resolve the issue.

This brings me to the high point of the wedding, and perhaps of Mary's modeling career. Mary, again fully confident that the Father wanted Jesus to resolve the issue there and then, turned to the waiters and said, "Do whatever he tells you" (John 2:5).

These words have directed Christians to her Son for two thousand years and represent one of Mary's greatest gifts to the world, one of her greatest acts of charity. In this brief statement, Mary proclaims from the rooftop the most important lesson we can learn on this earth: Turn to Christ and do what he asks. We are woefully incomplete as human beings without Jesus in our lives. We cannot know true happiness or develop a sense of fulfillment without following him and the mission he has in store for us. We will never become whole again and united with God the Father without accepting the gift of Mary's Son and embracing his redemptive work on the cross. We have so few words from Mary recorded in the Gospels, but she managed to say so much that day: "Do whatever he tells you."

In our ministry with young people, we need to imitate Mary. As apostles to the young, we draw near and join them along the path of their lives; we make sure our radar is up and that we are aware of their needs; we engage them in conversations about what is important to them; we commit to humbly serving them in whatever ways God asks of us; and we build healthy relationships with them and help to open their hearts to the gift of faith. But if we do not bring them to Jesus, we are not doing what we have been called to do. "Do whatever he tells you."

The next stop on our journey with Mary is at the foot of the cross. Rather than looking up to Jesus in this moment, I would like to look across to Mary Magdalene. Jesus' Mother must have been a tremendous source of encouragement in this woman's life. I am sure that as a part of the group of women disciples who traveled with Jesus and addressed his needs and those of the apostles, these two crossed paths often enough throughout Jesus' public ministry. However, they were particularly close companions at the crucifixion.

There remains debate in the Church over Mary Magdalene's true identity—whether she was a prostitute, the woman known as a sinner who enters the Pharisee's house and lavishes tears and perfume upon our Savior's feet, or even the sister of Martha and Lazarus. Without choosing to resolve that question, we do know from the Gospels that Jesus cast out seven demons from her (see Mark 16:9). The exact meaning of this reality is not clear; it may be that Jesus literally cast out seven demons, or it may be that she was afflicted with a very serious psychological ailment.

Regardless, we can safely assume that Mary from Magdala was lovingly healed by Jesus in a very powerful way from some serious illness and that, as always, it included the spiritual healing that flows from the forgiveness of sins. This healing led to a love for our Lord and a faith in him that was exceptional. She stood by him at the cross when eleven of his apostles were nowhere to be found. She was the first to the tomb at dawn on Easter Sunday and spent much of that morning weeping because Jesus was no longer in the tomb and was, at first, nowhere to be found. Then, she was the first, according to Scripture, to encounter the risen Lord and the first disciple to proclaim the Resurrection— to the apostles, no less. For these reasons and more, Pope Francis recently raised the Church's liturgical celebration of Mary Magdalene's entrance into heaven from a memorial to a feast day, on par with the twelve apostles.

I would like to posit that Mary participated with her Son in the ongoing healing process for Mary Magdalene. In this service, the Virgin Mary demonstrates the great place in God's heart for those who are hurting, those on the fringe of society, those who are possessed by demons. The scene depicted so often in Christian art with Mary, John, and Mary Magdalene at the foot of the cross proclaims to the world the importance of reaching out with the love of Christ to those carrying the heavy crosses of physical, mental, and spiritual illnesses.

Before we leave the scene of the cross, let us angle our gaze just a few degrees to focus on St. John. He provides another moment in Mary's life of charity from which we can receive instruction. From the cross, Jesus entrusted his mother to John and John to his mother. John was the "beloved disciple" and likely the youngest of the apostles. He deeply loved the Lord and was the only apostle to remain with Jesus at the foot of the cross. So we know that Jesus left Mary in very good hands. Still, this new mission for Mary must have caught her off guard to some extent. She probably did not see this request coming from the hand of God.

From the foot of the cross, Mary teaches us to remain flexible as the Lord's servants. He may ask us to do the unexpected. I have certainly found the Lord to be full of surprises during my years as a consecrated member of Youth Apostles. My assignment after six years as a priest by the Bishop of Arlington to Fredericksburg, a town more than an hour away from my community's center in McLean, Virginia, was one of those moments for me. So was my election by my brothers as the General Director of Youth Apostles when I was forty years old. I had never in my wildest dreams thought of being asked to serve in that capacity. Charity demands flexibility and an openness to God's providential will.

> *"Hail, Holy Lady, Most Holy Queen, Mary Mother of God,*
> *who art a Virgin forever, chosen from heaven by the most*
> *holy Father, whom He consecrated with the most holy beloved*
> *Son and the Paraclete Spirit, in whom was and is all plenitude*
> *of grace and all good. Hail His palace. Hail His tabernacle.*
> *Hail His house. Hail His vesture. Hail His handmaid. Hail*
> *His mother and all you holy virtues, which by grace and*
> *illumination of the Holy Ghost may you pour into the hearts*
> *of the faithful, and may you make out of the faithless*
> *ones men faithful to God."*
> —Johannes Jorgensen, *St. Francis*, 154

DEVOTION TO MARY

St. John, as the lone apostle at the foot of the cross, represents the Church on that dark and tumultuous afternoon. As our Lord utters the words "behold your mother," he shares his precious mother with every person who will ever call him Lord and Savior. Mary is an extraordinary blessing in his life, and Jesus longs to pass that blessing along to us, his brothers and sisters, her children in the order of grace.

So, paying close attention to our Lord's dying words, and in imitation of St. John, we have the task of drawing near to Mary and taking her into our home. In short, we are invited to seek particular inspiration in the way she lives her life as the greatest disciple of Jesus, to marvel at the woman she is and the unequaled role she played in Jesus' work of redemption, to take refuge in her motherly embrace, and to turn to her for her powerful intercessory prayers.

Devotion to Mary down through the centuries has taken on many rich and inspiring forms. While never wanting to limit the numerous devotions to Mary, I will focus my reflection on four of them.

THE ANGELUS

Praying the Angelus is a wonderful way to begin the day. The four main stanzas or verses all flow from the Word of God, so it is a way to commence the day's toil by turning to the Lord through the Scriptures.

The angel of the Lord declared unto Mary, and she conceived by the Holy Spirit. Hail Mary . . .

This verse recalls that the gift of salvation is always God's initiative, everywhere. The angel comes announcing God's gift and offering to Mary the chance to share in its accomplishment. Salvation is not something that we earn through hard work, extra prayer, or clever ideas. It is, quite simply, a gift from God. So is the new day that he sets before us. We begin the day with genuine gratitude for the blessing of life and the chance to start anew. Each sunrise is a sign that God never tires of us, in spite of our sins and shortcomings. He delights in us and grants us the chance to begin again through the power of his mercy and the invitation to follow him with all our heart.

Behold the handmaid of the Lord. Be it done unto me according to your Word. Hail Mary . . .

Faith is an invitation from God. It demands a response to him. Jesus stands at the door of our hearts and knocks. Since the doorknob is only on our side, we have to open the door to him. Mary responded with a supreme act of humble, obedient love. She makes a total gift of herself to God. We beg for the grace this day to respond to Jesus generously, as Mary did.

And the Word was made flesh, and dwelt among us. Hail Mary . . .

Mary became a vessel in the hand of God. Her radical yes brought Christ into the world. She is *"Theotokos,"* or "God-bearer." When we say yes to God, great things happen. As we do so throughout the day, we have the privilege of imitating Mary and bringing Jesus into our little corner of the world. As we begin each new day, we ask for the grace to allow Jesus' light to shine through us into the shadows of a hurting world.

Pray for us, O Holy Mother of God, that we may be made worthy of the promises of Christ.

Mary loves to intercede with her Son on behalf of her adopted children. As the perfect disciple of Jesus and from the perspective of heaven, Mary knows very well what we need to remain close to her Son and to become perfect as our heavenly Father is perfect. It is a great thing to ask Mary to pray for us, our families, all who are dear to us, and for those who stand most in need of prayers this day.

Let us pray: Pour forth, we beseech you, O Lord . . .

The final prayer in the Angelus refers directly to the great mysteries of the birth, passion, and resurrection of Jesus and, in light of those events, beseeches the Lord to fill our hearts with his grace and bring us to the glory of the Resurrection. Another simple prayer that is on target!

> *"From Mary, we learn to surrender to God's will in all things. From Mary, we learn to trust when all hope seems gone. From Mary, we learn to love Christ her Son and the Son of God."*
> —St. John Paul II

THE ROSARY

I am thrilled that the Rosary is making a comeback as a prayer devotion in many circles in the Church today. For some years, many areas of the Church were in turmoil. Praying the Rosary was one of the numerous prayer practices and devotions, along with adoration of the Blessed Sacrament, that were set aside by many in the midst of the turmoil.

St. John Paul II's devotion to the Rosary and his regular encouragement of the faithful to pray it helped change the tide. The Polish pope's inspiration to add the luminous mysteries to the devotion was brilliant. By focusing on Jesus' three-year public ministry, the new set of mysteries effectively filled an awkward void in the saving work of Christ upon which we meditate while praying the Rosary. A return to studying the lives of the great saints, many of whom were deeply devoted to praying the Rosary, also pushed a return to the practice. And, of course, the natural and supernatural tug that draws us to Mary's side could not be squelched for long. I say, "Welcome back!" to a healthy devotion to Mary and the Rosary.

One fundamental grace connected to praying the Rosary is that it keeps the central mysteries of our faith before our minds and hearts for prayerful reflection. It will always serve this great purpose. Before the days when books were common and most Christians were educated enough to read, the Rosary was a simple way to make sure that we recall and meditate upon the most significant events in the life of Christ and his mother. The prolific use of stained glass windows in many churches served a similar purpose. Interestingly, I find that, for different reasons, the same need remains today for Christians all over the world. For instance, many Christian men and women in the Western world still struggle with taking the time to do good formational reading and pray in other settings with the sacred Scriptures. So, the Rosary retains its important place in popular devotion.

It would be an injustice to say that this prayer is simply a method of keeping the important mysteries of our Christian faith in front of us. Yes, praying the Rosary maintains a certain familiarity with the Annunciation, the scourging at the pillar, and the descent of the Holy Spirit. However, by the grace of the Holy Spirit and with the prayerful intercession of Mary, we also dive deeper into the beauty and meaning of these mysteries. If we make the effort to invest ourselves when praying and strive to truly ponder the great scriptural events at the heart of the Rosary, the Holy Spirit reveals new insights and subtly invites us to deeper levels of conversion. I can't count the number of times I have come back all sweaty from praying the Rosary while going for a run or a walk and grabbed a pen and sheet of paper to jot down a few notes on a new insight that came to me while engaged in this prayer.

I will conclude my brief comments on the Rosary by highlighting one more grace. This prayer has the potential to be a most powerful source of intercessory prayer. Mary knows better than anybody the sacred heart of Jesus. When it comes to seeking and doing the will of the heavenly Father, she is all in. It makes plenty of sense to bring our needs, the needs of our loved ones, and the needs of the Church to God through Mary's intercession. "The prayer of a righteous man has great power in its effects" (James 5:16). God has a long-standing history of responding to Mary's intercession.

"To recite the rosary is nothing other than
to contemplate the face of Christ with Mary."
—St. John Paul II

MARY, QUEEN OF APOSTLES

Though she was not formally one of the twelve men Jesus chose at the beginning of his ministry in Galilee for special training and service as apostles, one could argue that Mary was herself an apostle of Jesus. She was the first to say yes to his mission (the Annunciation). Mary was the first to present Jesus to the Jews (arrival of the shepherds in Bethlehem). She was the first to present Jesus to the Gentile world (arrival of the three magi). Mary was the first to bring Jesus from one town to another (the Visitation). Mary was not one of the twelve, but she was certainly sent by Christ to bear witness to him.

Furthermore, Mary had a mission to the twelve apostles that helped give rise to devotion to her under the title Queen of Apostles. At the wedding at Cana, Jesus' response to Mary when she brings the looming need of the newlyweds to him could be construed as a refusal or at least an objection. However, we know that Jesus and Mary are completely open to the will of the Father and immensely sensitive to the promptings of the Holy Spirit revealing that will. So there is not, in fact, any true disagreement or hesitation to submit to that will. Mary confidently presses the point with Jesus, who performs the first of what John the Evangelist called our Lord's "signs." It is interesting to note here that John concludes this event by saying, "and his disciples believed in him." Mary was intimately involved with Jesus' first miracle, which led to the birth of the apostles' faith. This is no small detail in John's account of this wedding celebration.

Now let's turn our attention to the story of another "birth." The familiar context is Mary and the apostles huddled in prayerful expectation during the time between the ascension of our Lord into heaven and the descent of the Holy Spirit on Pentecost. The presence of our Blessed Mother is mentioned very specifically by St. Luke in the Acts of the Apostles. The apostles had just witnessed the Ascension, returned to Jerusalem, and gathered in the Upper Room. In that famous gathering space, "All these with one accord devoted themselves to prayer, together with the women and Mary, the mother of Jesus, and with his brothers" (Acts 1: 14).

The full context is worth reviewing. The apostles and, indeed, all of Christ's followers have endured a whirlwind of astounding events, namely the passion, death, resurrection, post-resurrection appearances, and ascension of Christ to the right hand of the Father. Now they enter a period of waiting, which I am sure is hard for them. They are probably anxious to get going with the great project of spreading the Good News about Jesus of Nazareth. However, he has told them to wait in Jerusalem. As much as they want to get started, they also must sense that they are in fact still missing something important. They are not quite ready. So Mary's mere presence during those nine days is a huge comfort to the apostles. Her radical trust in her Son, her supreme confidence in the Father's plans, and her peaceful demeanor are an irreplaceable blessing for everyone in the Upper Room.

St. Luke mentions in particular that they devoted themselves to prayer. The apostles, Mary, the other female followers, and the "brothers" prayerfully prepared for the coming of the Holy Spirit. Mary, as we know, was a prayer warrior. Plus, the mother of our Savior had already been overshadowed by the Holy Spirit at the time of the Annunciation, having thus become the spouse of the

Holy Spirit. This qualified Mary for a unique role in assisting the apostles in their nine-day period of prayer and preparation for Pentecost, the coming of the Holy Spirit.

Let me make a final stop in this reflection at the book of Revelation. In John's famous vision of heaven, he recounts, "And a great portent appeared in heaven, a woman clothed with the sun, with the moon under her feet, and on her head a crown of twelve stars" (Revelation 12:1). The crown of twelve stars is unquestionably a reference to both the twelve apostles of the Lamb and the twelve tribes of Israel. In Mary's role as Queen of Heaven and Earth, the Lord wants to highlight that she is Queen of Apostles.

In summary, Mary was, among her various roles, sent by God to bring Christ into the world, and so we could say she was an apostle. Additionally, she played a crucial role in the birth of Jesus, the birth of faith in the apostles, and the birth of the Church at Pentecost. For these reasons, the Church's tradition and devotion have granted the Mother of Jesus the title Mary, Queen of Apostles.

To conclude, we who have discerned a call from Christ to focus our apostolic energies on welcoming and accompanying young people—indeed, we who are apostles to youth—should find a special place in our heart for this devotion to Mary. She finds great joy in presenting Christ to us in the manger for prayerful meditation, keeping us focused on lovingly, obediently following him wholeheartedly ("Do whatever he tells you"), and preparing our hearts for a new outpouring of the Holy Spirit that sends us out to evangelize young people. Mary, Queen of Apostles, pray for us!

MARY, HELP OF CHRISTIANS

As Jesus' brothers and sisters who have come to love Mary, we cannot help but rejoice whenever we ponder her assumption into heaven and the countless blessings that came with that gift of God. She is united in a glorious and definitive way with her Son, Jesus, as well as with the Father and in the Holy Spirit. This gift of being drawn up into the very life and love of the Holy Trinity is possible because of the incarnation, passion, death, and resurrection of her precious Son. Mary now knows the fulfillment of all our deepest longings promised by the Lord: "What no eye has seen, nor ear heard, nor the heart of man conceived, what God has prepared for those who love him" (1 Corinthians 2:9). She gazes upon the very face of God and enjoys a place at the eternal banquet in heaven along with all the angels and saints. She joins the heavenly chorus that sings God's praises and worships him for all eternity. So, my heart overflows with joy as I ponder the Blessed Mother enjoying these blessings.

Something else fabulous happened on the day of the Assumption. The motherly care and powerful intercession that Mary offered the apostles and the other disciples of Jesus, especially John, have taken on a whole new dimension. They are no longer limited in time and space as they were during her earthly pilgrimage. Now, since Mary is in heaven and exists outside the limits of time and place, her ministry as queen mother has a universal scope.

This is an enormous, incalculable gift to the Church. It would be almost impossible to count the number of Christians who have taken refuge in Mary's loving arms for two thousand years; the miracles of healing, conversion, and protection that have been attributed to her intercession; the magnitude of hurting souls and nations to whom she has appeared offering encouragement and wisdom; and the confused pilgrims she has lovingly led to encounter her Son. Mary is indeed one of Jesus' most precious gifts to us!

One devotion with ancient roots that beautifully invites us to focus on this spiritual practice of turning to Mary for her unique intercession is Mary, Help of Christians.

Devotion to Mary under this title has a long history in the Church. St. John Chrysostom used it in a homily in 345 AD. Pope Pius V attributed an enormous and unexpected victory in a battle at sea that was crucial to turning back Muslim invasions of Europe in 1571 to Mary's intercession; consequently, he inserted the title into the famous Marian litany of Loreto. Pope Pius VII established the feast of Our Lady, Help of Christians on May 24, the day of his triumphal return to Rome after being arrested by Napoleon and detained as a prisoner for six years. A little closer to home, St. John Bosco and his Salesian community embraced this devotion and helped spread it around the world.

With the assistance of his own mother, St. John Bosco developed a very deep dedication to Mary that over time focused on this particular devotion. His dedication to Mary was greatly impacted by a dream that took place around the age of nine. The dream went like this:

He found himself in a large yard with a crowd of children playing. Some were laughing, others playing games and still others were cursing. Little John jumped into the midst to stop the cursing with feisty words and fists. A distinguished man dressed

in a white cloak and very radiant to behold appeared, called John
by name and asked him to take charge of the kids. "You will win
these friends of yours not with blows but with gentleness and love.
So start right now to teach them about the ugliness of sin and the
preciousness of virtue." The children had all gathered around the
one that spoke. "I will give you a lady teacher. Under her guidance
you can become learned. Without her all learning becomes fool-
ishness." St. John goes on to say, "At that moment I saw beside him
a lady of majestic bearing, dressed in a mantle that sparkled all
over . . . she beckoned me to come closer to her and took me kindly
by the hand." All of the children vanished and in their place were
goats, dogs, bears and other animals. "This is your field. This is
where you must work. Make yourself humble, sturdy and strong."

The wild animals appeared as gentle lambs. All of them were
frisking about and bleating, as if to welcome the man and the
woman.

The saint began to cry and begged the lady to please speak plainly
so that he could understand. She then placed her hand on his head
and said, "In due time you will understand everything."

St. John Bosco came to understand that these two figures were
Jesus and Mary. They were calling him to the service of youth and
planting the seeds of a new approach to this service that would be
called St. John Bosco's Preventive System.

The saint from Turin, Italy, grew to love Mary very deeply.
He turned to her constantly for her intercession in his various
ministries. He knew that the young boys and girls in his care

needed Mary to be their mother as well. He shared his love for her, preached about her often, taught about her role in Jesus' life and work, and encouraged the young people to seek refuge in her tender arms. When the apostle to youth decided to build a great church to function as the mother church of his congregation, he dedicated the masterpiece to Mary, Help of Christians (*Santa Maria Ausiliatrice* in Italian).

Over the years, St. John Bosco's ministry was marked by a wide range of miracles, including miracles of healing, multiplication of food for the boys, foreknowledge of future events, and gifts of money to cover bills that were due or long past due. These unexplained events were countless in number.

Toward the end of his life, he spoke of those miracles. "For the last ten years a report has been spreading, and the newspapers publish it, that Don Bosco works miracles. What a mistake! Don Bosco does not work miracles. He prays for himself and gets others to pray for those who recommend themselves to him; and that is all. As for miracles, it is the Blessed Virgin who works them. She sees Don Bosco needs money to feed and bring up his thousands of children as Christians; then she brings him benefactors by the favours she showers upon them" (Blessed John Bosco, A. Auffrey, S.C., Burns Oates & Washbourne LTD., 1930, p. 209).

St. John Bosco is a most powerful model of a person who devoted his whole life to the generous, humble, prayerful, and most effective service of young people. His whole life is worth imitating, including his devotion to Mary, Help of Christians.

CONCLUSION

The Church's exploration of the role Mary played in her Son's mission of redeeming the world, the outstanding example of her Christian way of life, and the ongoing role she plays in salvation history are vast and rich. I bow humbly before the great faith and wisdom of the Church and the saints with regard to their devotion to Mary. I humbly leave these four reflections, hoping they might be of assistance to those whom God has called to welcome and accompany young people to live Christlike lives based upon the Lord's sacrificial love.

> "... precisely because Mary is with God and in God,
> she is very close to each one of us. While she lived on this
> earth she could only be close to a few people. Being in God,
> who is actually 'within' all of us, Mary shares in this closeness
> to God. [Our Lady] knows our hearts, can hear our prayers,
> can help us with her motherly kindness. She always listens
> to us and, being Mother of the Son, participates in the power
> of the Son and in his goodness. We can always entrust
> the whole of our lives to this Mother."
> —Pope Emeritus Benedict XVI

CHAPTER 5

JESUS AND HIS SOLDIER SAINT

"In fact, the call to the new evangelization
is first of all a call to conversion."
—St. John Paul II, CELAM,
Dominican Republic, October 12, 1992

Christians living two thousand years after the birth of Christ have one fantastic advantage over the earliest Christians: We can look back and see how God has raised up numerous wonderful saints, men and women of deep faith in Jesus and exceptional zeal for spreading his light. The saints always blossom in a historical context, but they also become a source of tremendous grace for countless Christians down through the centuries. St. Ignatius of Loyola is one of those great saints.

God took Ignatius' intense passion for chivalrous military service to the King of Spain and transformed it into a zeal for being a soldier for Christ. St. Ignatius' marvelous conversion led to a love for Christ the king and a fresh new perspective on radically living the Gospel that quickly drew avid followers. He formed these followers into the Society of Jesus, the Jesuits, who became an army of men in the service of the king and his vicar on earth, the Pope. These spiritual soldiers were committed to surrendering their lives completely to the Lord and his call, freeing themselves from all distractions and attachments, doing everything for the greater glory of God, educating the world, especially her young, with the truths of our faith, and being at the disposal of the Pope.

As it happens, Ignatius arrives on the world scene at the time of the Protestant Reformation, which had seismic effects on the Catholic Church. It is an understatement to say that the Catholic Church was shaken as if by an earthquake during these years. This is not the place for a detailed analysis of the repercussions of Martin Luther and the posting of the Ninety-five Theses in 1517, which is considered to be the start of the Reformation. However, for the sake of context, I humbly submit that these realities resulted from the earthquake: the formal schism from the One, Holy, Catholic and Apostolic Church; the bold call into question of her capacity to teach infallibly in the name of Christ on issues of faith and morals; the casting aside of various teachings, practices, and sacraments by Luther, Calvin, Zwingli, and other leaders of the Reformation; and of course, the unwillingness to work out differences, even serious ones, from within the Church.

Ignatius and his Society of Jesus became a major force in the Counter-Reformation, the Church's response to the great schism. Their zeal for Christ, commitment to teaching the true faith, meteoric growth in numbers, and complete availability and obedience to the Pope proved to be an invaluable assistance to Christ and his Church during these tumultuous years.

The renewal that Ignatius helped bring about in the Church was fundamentally tied to a new spirituality that the former soldier gave to the Church based upon his own conversion experience and the focus on completely surrendering one's life to

Christ and his will for our lives. The Ignatian spirituality has proven enormously effective through our own day. To those who accompany young people in the twenty-first century, I offer a brief reflection on several of its key elements as a well-worn route to a strong life in Christ.

DEEP CONVERSION OF HEART

Ignatius' personal conversion is a spectacular work of Christ. It remains to this day one of the most significant elements of any discussion on Ignatius and his impact on the world and the Church.

Ignatius was born and raised in the castle of Loyola, the home of a noble family in the Basque Country of northern Spain. He was baptized Inigo but later changed his name to Ignatius, a derivative of Inigo that he thought would be more acceptable to foreigners, especially those from France and Italy. He was the youngest of thirteen children. His mother died soon after his birth and he was raised by the local blacksmith's wife. At a young age, Ignatius became a page of the courts in the service of a relative. As an educated young aristocrat growing up among the courtiers of the early 1500s, Ignatius dreamed of being a valiant soldier, dedicated to the heroic service of the King of Spain. He did in fact become a soldier, at the age of seventeen, and quickly began to strut around wearing his cape and flashing his sword and dagger. He had a famous encounter with a Muslim who denied the divinity of Christ. While not at this point very serious about his faith, he still considered this an affront. So Ignatius challenged the Moor to a duel and ran him through with his sword.

On April 20, 1521, at the age of thirty, while valiantly fighting in a battle against the French at the fortress of Pamplona, Ignatius was struck by a cannonball, damaging one leg and breaking the other. Severely wounded, he was carried by the French, who were impressed with his valor, to the castle of Loyola, where he remained for a long period of recuperation. While convalescing, Ignatius asked for popular novels to read about chivalry and knights in battle. None were to be found in the castle, so he settled for reading what was available: a book on the life of Christ and one on the lives of the saints. He particularly dove into *Vita Christi*, a commentary on the life of Christ by Ludolph of Saxony, which influenced the rest of his life. God began to work on his heart through this reading and reflection. Ignatius started to daydream of becoming a knight dedicated to the service of Jesus, the King of Kings, in imitation of the great saints such as Francis of Assisi and Dominic.

When Ignatius was finally able to walk, he took off on a riveting adventure filled with life-changing moments. He left immediately for the Benedictine monastery of Santa Maria de Montserrat, located in a breathtaking spot high on the cliffs a mountain, where he famously surrendered his sword before the well-known image of Our Lady of Montserrat. From there, he traveled by foot to the town of Manresa and spent nearly a year there on an extended retreat. For lodging, he went back and forth between a Dominican priory and a nearby secluded cave.

During this time, Ignatius dedicated himself to intense prayer, penance, and fasting. In the beginning, he experienced tremendous spiritual consolation and rejoiced in the new life he had chosen. He spent much time praying with the Gospels and focusing on the life of Christ.

At times, Ignatius also found himself slipping back into daydreaming about knight errantry and pursuing beautiful women of the courts of Spain, a thought pattern that remained rather attractive to him. In time, he noticed something very different about these thoughts of heroic battles and beautiful women. While the thoughts were naturally attractive and enjoyable for a brief moment, they soon left him feeling empty and unsatisfied. However, when he pondered giving his life over to Christ the king and following his commands, he noticed a joy and a peace that lasted beyond the initial consolation and continued to lift him up. The deeper peace and longer-lasting joy that flows from pondering and doing things for the glory of God became one tool in Ignatius' tool box used in the complicated and delicate process of discernment of spirits—a key element of the Spiritual Exercises.

For a period of time during this extended retreat, Ignatius experienced the most aggressively intense period of spiritual desolation. He was plagued by doubts, fears, and depression. There were moments of unforgettable darkness and despair that tempted him to abandon the project of becoming a soldier for Christ. During that bleak period, none of the usual practices—prayer, fasting, and acts of penance—proved immediately helpful. Ignatius found the grace to hang on to God and to persevere in prayer in spite of the darkness. The Lord eventually pulled him out of this time of despair, and he continued to progress along the path of deep conversion.

Ignatius took notes throughout his extended period of conversion at Manresa; they became the foundation of his Spiritual Exercises, a four-week retreat that he prepared for his brothers and many others who were open to a rich, transformative retreat experience. It remains one of the greatest gifts Ignatius offered the Church because it proclaims God's capacity to capture our hearts, change our lives, purify our desires, and call us to use a combination of natural and supernatural gifts to serve the king in marvelous ways.

> *"It is precisely because sin exists in the world, which 'God so loved . . . that he gave his only Son' (115), that God who 'is love' (116) cannot reveal himself otherwise than as mercy."*
> —St. John Paul II, *Dives in misericordia*, 13

SPIRITUAL FREEDOM

Do you ever get frustrated with yourself over your failure to avoid certain sins or to develop a longed-for virtue? Our Christian faith deals directly with this common experience.

The impact of original sin on every human being since our first parents is immeasurable. That fateful "No!" deeply damaged the human nature we inherited from Adam and Eve. In Christ we have our remedy. It starts with the precious gift of baptism. So we rejoice heartily in the gift of baptism, with its abundant graces and glorious effects. Baptism wipes away the stain of original sin, restores us to original grace, makes us children of God, transforms us into temples of the Holy Spirit, and welcomes us as members of the Church. Baptism gives God's children abundant graces, which flow from the cross, the tree of life.

However, many of the effects of original sin remain in us. Our human nature, even following baptism, remains dented. Traditionally, the Church calls this lingering effect of original sin concupiscence. Consequently, we are not so quick to choose the good in our lives. Our vision of reality and our capacity to live in the light of Christ remain hazy. We are terribly prone to bad habits and to an ugly selfishness, which enslave us and keep us from enjoying the new life we have in Christ. We are often governed by a pride that keeps us from being aware of our need for God and drives us to seek a false sense of freedom.

St. Ignatius gives us a tool to assist us in this battle with the effects of original sin. He was dogged in his efforts to help fellow pilgrims live in the freedom of Christ. Consequently, one of the principal goals of Ignatian spirituality is the concept of spiritual freedom. To be truly free is to be free from attachments to anything on this earth that keeps us from loving God with every ounce of our being. The path to this freedom takes us through three gardens: embracing our purpose in life, Ignatian indifference, and inordinate attachments.

> *"God is the source of all goodness and man remains free only*
> *in so far as he remains close to the Lord."*
> (Youth Apostles General Statutes, 1.26)

A CLEAR UNDERSTANDING OF OUR PURPOSE

A few years ago, I read a book called *Good to Great,* by Jim Collins. He helped lead a team of bright analysts in a study of companies that were successful over the long haul. They were trying to answer the question of why some companies make the leap to greatness and others do not. One clear reality that stood out among the study group members was that all of the good-to-great companies had a "hedgehog" concept—a simple, clear understanding of who they were and what they were doing. It was not a goal, strategy, or plan, but an understanding. The good-to-great companies were able to translate that understanding into a simple, crystalline concept.

Ignatius, in fact, begins his Spiritual Exercises by stating most clearly who we are and what we are doing on this earth. "Man is created to praise, reverence, and serve God our Lord, and by this means to save his soul" (23).

The most important things in life need to be stated and restated. Not all of us have actually embraced this understanding of our existence and made it a focal point for our lives. Even for those who have, it is incredibly easy to get distracted by smaller goals in our lives and countless other demands that are urgent but not critical in the long run. We can get so caught up in the significant efforts required to get through the day that we gradually lose sight of the most important goal: to love God above all things in our lives—to praise, reverence, and serve him.

This very critical understanding of our purpose drives the whole rest of Ignatius' Spiritual Exercises. It is the foundation of this thirty-day retreat—and of the whole Christian life.

> *"Man is created to praise, reverence, and serve God*
> *our Lord, and by this means to save his soul."*
> —St. Ignatius, *Spiritual Exercises*, 23

IGNATIAN INDIFFERENCE

After establishing a clear understanding of our purpose on this earth and inviting a new, radical commitment to it, Ignatius proceeds to develop a strategy for accomplishing this purpose. In its essence, it is quite simple: All of creation and all of God's gifts and blessings are to be used insofar as they assist us on the path to accomplishing this purpose. All things that get in the way should be removed from our lives. Ignatius remained so focused on this purpose for our lives that he lived with and encouraged a tremendous indifference to everything in the world.

"For this it is necessary to make ourselves indifferent to all created things in all that is allowed to the choice of our free will and not prohibited to it; so that, on our part, we want not health rather than sickness, riches rather than poverty, honor rather than dishonor, long rather than short life . . ." (*Spiritual Exercises*, 23).

Ignatius truly did not desire health over sickness, wealth over poverty, long life over short, easy life over difficult . . . I think you get the point. What reigned over all was "to praise, reverence, and serve God our Lord."

During the exercises, Ignatius offers a meditation that further explains this concept of indifference. It is commonly referred to as the "three degrees of humility." The first kind of humility is necessary for eternal salvation. "I so lower and humble myself, as much as is possible to me, that in everything I obey the law of God, so that . . . I would not be in deliberation about breaking a Commandment, whether Divine or human, which binds me under mortal sin" (David L. Fleming, S.J., *The*

Spiritual Exercises of St. Ignatius, 165). In other words, I live my life so as to never consciously choose to commit a mortal sin.

The second kind of humility is more perfect than the first. "I find myself at such a stage that I do not want, and feel no inclination to have, riches rather than poverty, to want honor rather than dishonor, to desire a long rather than a short life—the service of God our Lord and the salvation of my soul being equal; and so not for all creation, nor because they would take away my life, would I be in deliberation about committing a venial sin" (Fleming, 166). In other words, I desire to follow God and his will so dearly that I do not want to turn away from him even in the smallest of ways. I do not even want to commit a venial sin.

The third kind of humility is the most perfect: "when—including the first and second, and the praise and glory of the Divine Majesty being equal—in order to imitate and be more actually like Christ our Lord, I want and choose poverty with Christ poor rather than riches, opprobrium with Christ replete with it rather than honors; and to desire to be rated as worthless and a fool for Christ, Who first was held as such, rather than wise or prudent in this world" (Fleming, 167). My love for Christ is so strong that I want to be right there with him in his poverty, insults, and revilement. I prefer those things to being esteemed as wise or prudent by the world. This, indeed, is a most radical form of Christ-inspired indifference.

Perhaps this meditation is a little shocking to you. It is incredibly challenging; it stirs my heart and humbles me every time I ponder it. The real question for us is not what kind of humility we are practicing right now, but are we willing to be on the path of growing in humility?

> *"In 1942—I wanted to give Jesus something without*
> *reserve—With the permission of my Confessor I made*
> *a vow to God—binding under mortal sin—to give to God*
> *anything that He may ask—'Not to refuse Him anything.'"*
> —St. Teresa of Calcutta (Brian Kolodiejchuk,
> *Mother Teresa: Come Be My Light,* 191)

INORDINATE ATTACHMENTS

Ignatius offers another very helpful meditation, which helps keep us focused on and assists us with accomplishing what is most important. He invites us to prayerfully discern the existence of inordinate attachments in our lives. These are people, activities, and interests (anything, honestly) that distract us in large or small ways from our principal purpose. It is easy to grasp that our sins and selfish attitudes represent inordinate attachments in our lives—angry outbursts, turning to pornography, neglecting an aging parent or a difficult sibling, refusing to pray, sexual encounters outside of marriage, etc.

However, Ignatius, in keeping with his passion for following Christ completely, wants to dive much deeper. There are also people, activities, and interests in our lives that are neutral or even positive in and of themselves, but that can still become obstacles to our great purpose in life. These include exercise, hobbies, social media, volunteering to serve the homeless, etc. In these instances, even though they may be good for us in a broader, generic sense, they become inordinate for us in this moment if we allow them to keep us from doing God's more perfect will, surrendering our heart completely to the Lord, or keeping our eyes fixed on Jesus. For instance, if I go to the homeless shelter every Saturday to serve lunch but never visit my aging parent who lives across town, I am missing the mark. If I exercise forty minutes every day and keep my body in great shape but do not take time for daily prayer and keeping my soul in shape, I am missing the mark.

The process of discerning our inordinate attachments is not always easy. We need God's gentle light as well as honesty, prayer, and openness to the guidance of the Holy Spirit. Retreats often provide the environment where we are more open and attentive to the promptings of the Holy Spirit and the insights he provides regarding our attachments. Of course, a good spiritual director who knows us well can be invaluable in this process. Brothers and sisters in an intentional community or small faith group can also help us by pointing out areas of our lives where we might be blind to what is obvious or how God is acting in our lives.

Returning regularly to this honest meditation is really helpful for advancing in faith. Sometimes old attachments can unexpectedly return. Sometimes new attachments can creep into our lives. Being open to the reality of these attachments is one thing; being dedicated to making progress in rooting them out of our lives is another. St. Ignatius of Loyola, pray for us!

"And he said to him, 'You shall love the Lord
your God with all your heart, and with all
your soul, and with all your mind.'"
(Matthew 22:37)

THE CALL OF CHRIST

Unquestionably, some of the most inspiring and powerful passages in the Gospels and in the Acts of the Apostles involve the call that Jesus extends to his apostles and disciples. From the many, those of Matthew, Peter, Paul, and the woman at the well stand out.

Allow me to turn to a classic work of art to illustrate the beauty of one outstanding moment in the Gospels: Caravaggio's famous painting *The Calling of Saint Matthew*, which hangs in the Church of St. Louis of the French in Rome. Matthew lived daily with the social and religious repercussions of his profession as a tax collector. In the eyes of most Jews, tax collection was a heinous profession, and it meant being ostracized from nearly every circle of Jewish interaction, in particular the synagogue. Any public practice of the Jewish faith was all but impossible. When Jesus approached Matthew, the tax collector most likely felt a sense of unworthiness. In Caravaggio's great work, the surprise on Matthew's face is captivating. The look also includes a strong mix of wonder, as if he's saying, "Who am I that you would step into my office?" Matthew is making a gesture with his hand that speaks loudly as well: His forefinger is dramatically pointing to and accusing himself.

The figure of Jesus is central to the painting. Our Lord's hand is extended to Matthew in a way that resembles God the Father's hand in Michelangelo's painting on the ceiling of the Sistine Chapel. This is a clear reference to the notion that Jesus is offering to Matthew in this moment the chance to be re-created. A window looming above the characters in the scene has four panes, which take on the conspicuous shape of a cross. Jesus is offering to Matthew a brand-new life and an awesome mission that are the fruit of the future cross of Jesus.

The countenance of Jesus is also a central feature of this masterpiece. On his face there is strength, conviction, and focus. This is not a random, thoughtless act on Jesus' part. He wants Matthew on his team. His call and his forgiveness are real. "Come follow me!"

Matthew's response was immediate, if not surprising: "And he rose and followed him" (Matthew 9:9). Then he proceeded quickly to offer a wonderful gift to Jesus—a meal at his house with all his friends. To the dismay of the Pharisees, Jesus was thrilled to have time with and offer countless graces to this crowd of sinners and outcasts: "'I desire mercy, and not sacrifice.' For I came not to call the righteous, but sinners" (Matthew 9:13).

With this great Gospel event in mind, Ignatius dedicates all of week two of the Spiritual Exercises to the call of Christ. Indelibly imprinted on his mind is his own conversion experience, in which Jesus made a dramatic entrance into his own life, offered the overwhelming gift of his mercy, and extended a personal invitation to give up his old way of life and follow him. Ignatius was absolutely convinced that Jesus continues to encounter his disciples in powerful ways and extend to them a personal invitation to participate in the mission of building his kingdom on this earth. He was compelled by the need to assist others in having this personal encounter with Christ that affirms his saving love and gives him the opportunity to look them in the eye and say, "Follow me."

Ignatius offers a variety of Gospel passages for meditation at this stage in the exercises, including the stories of the Nativity, the presentation in the Temple, the finding of the child Jesus in the Temple, our Lord's temptations in the desert, the call of the apostles, and the eight Beatitudes. In addition, he personally crafted several meditations for use during this second week, including the two standards, the three degrees of humility, and three types of persons. Let's glance at his reflection on the two standards.

Drawing once again on his previous experience, Ignatius turns to the familiar image of the military standard. Each army fighting in a battle has a standard, a flag that goes before the troops in a battle. It plays a very significant role for the soldiers, functioning as a continual point of reference during the fight, a rallying point, a source of inspiration, and an indication of progress or failure. The standard is usually planted in a significant place at the end of a battle to proclaim the victor. The famed statue of soldiers at Iwo Jima in Washington, D.C., is an enduring image of the power of the standard.

Ignatius starts by examining the standard of Satan. But first he suggests, as always, to begin the meditation by praying for a particular grace: "I ask for the gift of being able to recognize the deceits of Satan and for the help to guard myself against them; and also I ask for knowledge of the true life exemplified in Jesus Christ, my Lord and my God, and the grace to live my life his way" (*Spiritual Exercises*, 139).

He proceeds to set the scene by encouraging us to imagine Satan, "the chief of all the enemy," sitting on a throne, surrounded by fire and smoke and inspiring "horror and terror." Then we are encouraged to consider how Satan summons his troops, the demons, and scatters them from city to city throughout the world, allowing no location, state in life, or individual to be overlooked.

Finally, Ignatius poses for reflection that Satan goads the demons to lay snares for men to bind them in chains. Satan's efforts focus on three snares: coveting earthly riches, attaining worldly honor, and developing "overweening pride."

Next Ignatius asks us to ponder the standard of Christ, which is in stark contrast to that of Satan. First, consider Jesus, who is standing in a lowly place in a great plain near Jerusalem and whose appearance is "beautiful and attractive" (*Spiritual Exercises*, 144). Then ponder how the King of Kings chooses a multitude of followers from every state in life and from each form of service in the Church and sends them out to every corner of the world to spread the Good News to all.

Christ our Lord also makes an address to the servants and friends whom he enlists for this enterprise. First, he recommends that they be committed "to seek to help all, first by attracting them to the highest spiritual poverty, and should it please the Divine Majesty, and should deign to choose them for it, even to actual poverty." After that, Ignatius challenges them to embrace "a desire for insults and contempt, for from these spring humility. . . . Hence, there will be three steps: the first, poverty as opposed to riches; the second, insults or contempt as opposed to the honor of this world; the third, humility as opposed to pride. From these three steps, let them lead men to all other virtues" (*Spiritual Exercises*, 146).

Have I firmly chosen to follow one standard or another? Have I followed Christ into battle, or am I watching from a distance?

*"And passing along by the Sea of Galilee, he saw Simon
and Andrew the brother of Simon casting a net in the sea;
for they were fishermen. And Jesus said to them, 'Follow
me and I will make you become fishers of men.' And
immediately they left their nets and followed him."*
(Mark 1:16–18)

AD MAJOREM DEI GLORIAM

The fire of the Holy Spirit worked hard on Ignatius' heart and
soul. He was not content with simply doing things for the glory
of God; rather, he was focused on doing them for the *greater* glory
of God. Ignatius did not want to follow God's will in any generic
sense, doing some things throughout the day that we know are
usually pleasing to God; rather, he wanted to be completely committed to doing exactly what God wanted at every moment of
the day.

For instance, Ignatius was not satisfied with the enormous
challenge of preaching the fullness of the Christian faith to the
people of Europe in the wake of the Protestant Reformation—in
addition, he greatly desired to go to the Holy Land and convert
the Muslims. Ignatius was not only committed to sending his
brother Jesuits to neighboring countries in Europe for the spread
of the Gospel; he also sent one of his closest collaborators and
his dearest friend, Francis Xavier, to evangelize in the Far East,
where he converted some fifty thousand Christians, mostly in
India and Japan. Ignatius sent him off on this missionary project
knowing that he may never see him again. In the end, St. Francis
Xavier died on an island just off the coast of China on his way to

begin a new mission in that vast land. It is not a coincidence that in the Jesuit Chiesa del Gesù in Rome, the remains of St. Ignatius are buried beneath an altar to the left side of the main altar, and the right arm of St. Francis Xavier decorates the altar directly across from him to the right of the main altar.

This commitment of St. Ignatius to dive deep into the will of God and give until we have no more to offer is often referred to as the "more" of Ignatius. He was not content with any hint of mediocrity or any acceptance of a lukewarm approach to the faith. He was constantly striving to give God the absolute best of himself and likewise to call others to stretch beyond what is commonly acceptable, what is the norm, in order to do all for the greater glory of God.

It is important to note that Ignatius' commitment to the "more" is not something he made up as some kind of overzealous soldier. It is the response of a saint to Jesus in the Gospels. Our Lord himself sets the tone for this magnanimous approach to life. Recall how Jesus taught his disciples to love their enemies and pray for their persecutors, to go an extra mile when a Roman soldier demands that you accompany him for one mile, to turn your other cheek when you are slapped on one side of the face, and to have the attitude of a slave in the humble service of your neighbor. I would argue that the most demanding of Jesus' commands is the greatest of them all: "This is my commandment, that you love one another as I have loved you" (John 15:12). Jesus wants us to grow in faith to the point that we learn to genuinely love those around us as he did. The call of the Christian is to live a Christlike life.

LOVE FOR THE CHURCH

In keeping with Ignatius' sense of the "more," and flowing from his chivalrous nature, the founder of the Jesuits developed in himself and incorporated into his early band of brothers a powerful love for the Church. He grasped that Christ had a world-changing mission that he shared with the Church: "Go therefore and make disciples of all nations, baptizing them in the name of the Father and of the Son and of the Holy Spirit, teaching them to observe all that I have commanded you; and lo, I am with you always, to the close of the age" (Matthew 28:19–20). This mission was entrusted to the Church with Peter and his successors at the head.

In the years following his conversion, Ignatius dedicated himself to getting a formal education in preparation for being ordained a priest and to building the foundation of the Jesuit order. During this time, which was complicated by the Protestant Reformation, he suffered a great deal of scrutiny at the hands of the Church. Numerous times he was detained, brought before the Inquisition, imprisoned, and told not to minister in the name of Christ by various Church leaders. He always humbly submitted to their demands. He actually looked upon these inquiries, imprisonments, and commands as ways for God to purify his soul and lead him to greater holiness.

Ignatius' love for the Church never faltered. In fact, it grew. In the end, he did not simply establish a community that is generically committed to being obedient to the Church and her visible head, the Pope; rather, the saint from Loyola and his Society of Jesus included a fourth vow in their constitution to go wherever the Pope should send them for the salvation of souls. In other words, they developed a special charism to be ready to go at the drop of a hat to serve a developing need of the Pope.

This commitment to being obedient to the Church—especially her visible head on earth, but also our local bishop—remains as important as ever in our own day. We are invited by the beautiful charism of Ignatius and his shining example to be loyal and obedient sons and daughters of the Pope and of our local bishop. This involves great trust—the Holy Spirit is indeed guiding the Pope and his ministry. It means respecting and following his clear directives, even when they do not represent our personal perspective. It means reading his writings and seeking to grasp and share his mind and heart for living the Gospel in our present day. It means giving him the benefit of the doubt when his preaching or actions do not make sense to us. It means trusting that God is in charge of the spread of his kingdom, and that he is faithful to his promise to remain with us until the end of time.

> *"See that you all follow the bishop, even as Jesus Christ*
> *does the Father, and the presbytery as you would the apostles;*
> *and reverence the deacons, as being the institution of God.*
> *Let no man do anything connected with the Church*
> *without the bishop. . . . Wherever the bishop shall appear,*
> *there let the multitude of the people also be; even as*
> *wherever Jesus Christ is, there is the Catholic Church."*
> —St. Ignatius of Antioch,
> *Letter to the Smyrnaeans*, Ch. 8

PRAYER CENTERED ON THE SCRIPTURES

Allow me to return briefly to a topic that I considered in chapter three in the section "The Table of God's Word." Ignatius bestowed on the world a strong challenge to center our prayer lives around prayerful meditation on the Scriptures, always giving priority to the Gospels. We will have no reason or motivation to do all things for the greater glory of God if we have not, through prayer and sacraments, come to love God above all things and to know in the depths of our soul a longing to share our greatest treasure with those who are near to us.

The truths, words, images, and events recorded in the sacred Scriptures, particularly in the New Testament, were recorded under the direct inspiration of the Holy Spirit. They contain a vast amount of riches that we can never exhaust. They are free for our consumption. We simply need to turn to them and learn the art of treasure hunting.

In this vein, but taking a slightly different angle, one reason why religious art, especially in Rome, is so inspiring to me is because the pieces that truly speak to the soul are the result of artists praying with the Scriptures. Many—arguably most—of the great painters, sculptors, and architects of the churches, chapels, and sacristies in Rome were men and women of faith in Jesus. They desired to give great glory to God through their artistic skills. With those artists who were not so faithful and had less pure motives, God used their superior talents regardless to produce great works that would inspire the faithful to draw closer to him and to lift up their hearts to praise him for his marvelous deeds.

For instance, there is a marble statue of Jesus with two children in the Church of St. Celia that depicts these children with a beautiful reverence for Christ and contagious joy at being in his presence. One boy is kneeling at Jesus' feet, holding a piece of his garment and kissing it. The girl is on her tippy toes, grabbing his leg and presumably saying, "Uppie!"—that is, "Lift me into your arms." Jesus' hand is on her head in a most affectionate touch. I am hard-pressed to think this statue was not conceived in prayer. It invites a faithful Christian to marvel, as Jesus commands, at the faith of his little ones and be committed to welcoming them and bringing them to his warm embrace.

Another terrific example of art inspired by the Scriptures is a painting in St. Peter's Basilica above an altar, where I was privileged to celebrate Mass several times, depicting the scene where Jesus invites Peter to walk on the water. The waves are really crashing about, the wind is blowing hard, the other eleven apostles are distracted and panic-stricken by the power of the storm, and Jesus has extended his hand to save Peter, who is sinking into the sea. One reflection that comes to my mind while pondering this masterpiece is that life is a huge storm and we are sunk without Jesus and his saving grace. I am moved to cry out with Peter, "Lord, save me" (Matthew 14:30).

We desperately need the nourishment of the Scriptures. St. Paul had this to say to the Christians in Rome: "For whatever was written in former days was written for our instruction, that by steadfastness and by the encouragement of the scriptures we might have hope" (Romans 15:4). Paul emphasizes that the Scriptures are given for instruction, steadfastness, and hope. Why would we turn down that assistance? And remember, we are spoiled today with how available the sacred Scriptures are to us in print and through the internet. There are tons of resources out there that make it easier than ever to pray with God's inspired Word. We have no excuse other than our lack of desire or discipline to pray with them each day.

> *"We need to help young people to gain confidence*
> *and familiarity with Sacred Scripture so it can become*
> *a compass pointing out the path to follow."*
> —Pope Benedict XVI, *Verbum domini*, 104

CONCLUSION

Saints are a living Gospel for the world to gaze upon. They find great inspiration in the Gospel way of life and are committed to faithfully walking this extraordinary and fulfilling path through life. They do so with quickness, joy, and consistency, in good times and bad. They remind us that being a true Christian is possible and they inspire us to get up when we have fallen down. For these basic reasons, the saints are always a shining light and are a tremendous blessing to the Church.

In addition, each of the canonized saints is graced by God to shine a spotlight on particular dimensions of the Gospel. This is what makes them unique. St. Francis of Assisi illuminated living an evangelical life of radical poverty and simplicity, the gift of living our faith in community, and the burning desire to share in the suffering of Christ. St. John Bosco was like the midday sun exposing the immense importance of relational ministry with young people, the necessity of serving them with the forged virtue of chastity and loving-kindness, and the conviction that deep inside, every young person wants to know and experience God. St. Thérèse of the Child Jesus taught the whole world to follow the little way, marked by complete trust in the Lord's love and mercy and the freedom that comes from letting Jesus lift us up in his gentle arms and carry us to heaven.

The life and teaching of St. Ignatius of Loyola, as we have already noted, shines a magnificent light on the grace of remaining focused on where we come from and where we are going, the Christian project of detaching ourselves from anything that keeps us from fully embracing God and his will for us, and the all-important process of discerning God's personal call. I shall conclude this chapter by highlighting one more great grace that Ignatius brings to the Church: his invitation to the whole world to embrace the Gospel precept of doing all things for the greater glory of God (*ad majorem Dei gloriam*).

CHAPTER 6

JESUS BESTOWS NEWNESS OF LIFE

*"I [John the Baptist] baptize you with water
for repentance, but he [Jesus] who is coming
after me is mightier than I, whose sandals
I am not worthy to carry; he will baptize you
with the Holy Spirit and with fire."*

—Matthew 3:11

Easter is a glorious time of the Church's liturgical year. We take
fifty days to joyfully celebrate Jesus' resurrection from the dead
and the brand-new life he shares with those who believe in him.
It begins by focusing on the unexpected yet transforming appearances of our risen Lord to his disciples. The encounters are warm
and personal, and they restore hope to his bruised band of followers.

It is evident in the Gospels that Jesus' closest collaborators
were an absolute mess following Good Friday. The scandal of the
cross had sucked the life out of them. In spite of several warnings
and clear references to Old Testament prophecies that were intended to prepare the world for his darkest hour, the passion of
Jesus crushed his followers. We too have moments of great desolation in our lives. We can get enormously worn down by life's

burdens and crosses. We too can reach a point where we wonder if we can take another step. There are moments when we don't see the light of God or feel the warmth of his love.

Our Lord's appearances are wonderfully renewing when we ponder them through eyes of faith. They include his sudden appearance to the apostles in the Upper Room on Easter Sunday night, his breakfast with them on the shore of the Sea of Galilee, his renewing and reassuring use of Mary Magdalene's name around the corner from the empty tomb, and his invitation to Thomas to place his hand into his pierced side. Our Lord's pastoral care for the leaders of his flock recounted at the conclusion of the four Gospels is a marvel to ponder in our hearts and proclaim to the world.

Yet these appearances were not the full story. The Lord's saving work was not yet complete. Something vastly important was missing. Jesus introduced this "something" at the Last Supper with words that must have stung the apostles: "Nevertheless I tell you the truth: it is to your advantage that I go away. . ." (John 16:7). There is absolutely no way they could fully comprehend the meaning of his words that evening. The thought of Jesus, whom they had given up everything to follow, going away so quickly had to seem like complete nonsense. Yet he had a plan that was earth-shattering, if not confusing at the start: "for if I do not go away, the Counselor will not come to you; but if I go, I will send him to you" (John 16:7).

It was God's providential plan for Jesus to leave. On the one hand, he had to suffer, die, and rise on the third day. This was the Father's will for the redemption of the world. On the other hand, it was upon the completion of those saving events that the

Father and the Son would pour forth the Holy Spirit upon the Church and the world. This gift of the Holy Spirit would, in fact, complete the saving work of the Father and the Son, completely transform the lives of his apostles and disciples, and set the world on fire.

The focus of the liturgy during the Easter season makes an important transition and turns to focus on the effects of these mysteries on the lives of Jesus' followers, particularly by looking at the Acts of the Apostles. Here, we are fed by the evangelist Luke's account of the life of the early Church, in which we see convicted and courageous apostles and disciples continuing the work of Christ through the Church. St. Paul, in his letter to the Romans, says, "We were buried therefore with him by baptism into death, so that as Christ was raised from the dead by the glory of the Father, we too might walk in newness of life" (Romans 6:4).

I would like to spend this chapter looking at this newness of life. How does it manifest itself in our lives and empower us to be brand-new creations and effective instruments in God's hands for the evangelization of young people?

> *"Now when they saw the boldness of Peter and John,*
> *and perceived that they were uneducated, common men,*
> *they wondered; and they recognized that they had been with*
> *Jesus. But seeing the man that had been healed standing*
> *beside them, they had nothing to say in opposition.*
> *But when they had commanded them to go aside out of the*
> *council, they conferred with one another, saying,*
> *'What shall we do with these men? For that a notable sign*
> *has been performed through them is manifest to all the*
> *inhabitants of Jerusalem, and we cannot deny it.'"*
>
> (Acts 4:13–16)

A RESPONSE IN TRUTH

1. EMBRACING THE TRUTH

Our prevailing culture does not like to admit that there exist in reality universal truths, some of which are built into our nature and the world around us by our Creator and some of which are revealed through his only begotten Son and the working of the Holy Spirit. Jesus spoke of this reality when addressing his disciples: "I am the way, the truth and the life; no one comes to the Father but by me" (John 14:6). To emphasize that the truths he came to reinforce and reveal were meant for the whole world because they are universally true, Jesus addressed this topic to Pontius Pilate, the Roman procurator: "For this I was born, and for this I have come into the world, to bear witness to the truth. Everyone who is of the truth hears my voice" (John 18:37).

Once we have come to know and love Jesus, these truths of our Catholic faith begin to make more and more sense. They gradually and inevitably lead us to true freedom and to more abundant life. Even when some of these truths are hard to grasp and put into practice, we do so with increasing joy because of the love we have for Jesus and because we see these truths bearing fruit in our lives.

In summary, Jesus is constantly seeking us out. Once we choose to engage, to let him draw close and show us his amazing mercy and love, we begin to experience new life in the Holy Spirit. This new life includes the commitment to remain at his feet. This strong relationship with our Lord leads us to warmly embrace all the truth that he revealed. We long, in fact, to be faithful to Christ and the Church that he instituted in order to hand on, safeguard, and continue to teach this beautiful truth in his holy name. A calm yet firm confidence in Jesus and all that he has revealed begins to reign in our hearts.

> *"For this I was born, and for this I have come*
> *into the world, to bear witness to the truth. Everyone*
> *who is of the truth hears my voice."*
> (John 18:37)

2. HANDING ON THE TRUTH

As a result of the disciples' firm confidence in Jesus, we, as apostles to young people, are able and committed to hand on this faith in the midst of our confused and rebellious culture. We desire to accompany them and teach them the fundamentals of the faith so that their lives, their prayer and worship, their decisions, and their social lives are gradually built upon the foundation that is Christ and the life of virtue that enables us to live out these truths.

St. John Bosco was convinced that the great teachings of our Christian faith are extremely attractive to young minds because they are true and good. They need to be presented in effective, relevant, and compelling ways so that young people make the personal choice to embrace them in freedom, not fear. These truths are meant to be revealed, discussed, pondered, and yes, fully embraced. But the teachings of our faith cannot be forced down the throats of the young. It is counterproductive to beat them over the head with such truths, making them out to be like weapons. Rather, our task as educators is to till the soil of their hearts so that they will embrace the seed of faith, allow it to grow deep roots, and produce an abundant harvest.

It is worth pointing out that Jesus exercised extraordinary patience with the crowds and with his disciples. He is our model for forming young hearts and minds. So often, the twelve apostles were obstinate, clueless, or just plain slow to grasp what Jesus was teaching them.

One particularly disheartening moment comes quickly to mind. Jesus offers one of his predictions about his looming suffering and death at the hands of certain Jewish leaders. Immediately after this prediction, the cohort departs for another town. When they arrive at the next town, Jesus asks them what they were discussing along the way. They fall silent, for they were discussing which of them was the greatest. This is a particularly dark, selfish moment for the apostles. I would have been tempted to fire this motley crew of twelve and hire another at that point. Jesus, however, uses this opportunity as a teaching moment, explaining one of his most critical lessons. Greatness in his kingdom means service. If you wish to be great, you must be willing to become a slave, the servant of all. Jesus' patience was extraordinary!

So Jesus teaches us apostles to young people that the most frustrating moments with our "disciples" are likely to be the best moments to teach truths and lessons that will sink deeply into their hearts. This approach to educating young people requires virtue, grace, and prayer.

One of the most critical ways we till the soil of the hearts of young people is by breaking open the Word of God with them on a regular basis. This is easy to do if we ourselves are spending the proper time in study and prayer with the Scriptures. Our love for the Word, our insights into its beauty, the ease with which we apply it to our lives, our capacity to see its connections with other passages and truths of the faith, and the example of our own prayer lives will help young people desire to pray with the Scriptures, accept the truths contained therein, and live by their high standards. This element of our service to young people will till the soil of their hearts, help to remove rocks and weeds, and assist God's Word to penetrate deeply into their lives.

> *"Each young person should be considered 'holy ground,'*
> *bearer of seeds of divine life, before which we must*
> *'take off our shoes' in order to draw near and enter*
> *more deeply into the Mystery."*
> —Pope Francis, *Christus vivit*, 67

3. TEACHING THEM TO PRAY

In a similar vein, young people will never authentically embrace the faith without drawing close to the Lord through the development of the discipline of prayer. It is only in the midst of that lived union with God that we can understand the faith and have the grace needed to live it. "It is only through closeness to God that mankind can remain faithful to the truth, and this closeness occurs through an enriched interior life, cultivated through prayer and the Sacraments" (Gaudium et spes, 1.18).

As a consequence, ministry to young people includes teaching them how to pray—and to love it. This process begins by providing them with plenty of opportunities for prayer. People normally learn to pray from experience. It is important to include a variety of forms of prayer.

Since the Eucharist is the source and summit of our Christian lives, the Mass deserves focused attention. We clearly must draw upon the rich teaching of the Church regarding the meaning and beauty of this supreme sacrament. We also have the witness and reflections of the saints, which can be most inspiring and informative. In addition, it is very helpful to explain over time the history and meaning of the different parts of the Mass, including the various prayers and gestures. When done well, these explanations can help the Mass really come alive for young and old alike. Priests who clearly love the Mass, are able to patiently explain its beauty, and enjoy working with young people can be an enormous blessing in our service to them. Teaching Masses, explanations in the chapel before the Mass, and occasional smaller Masses celebrated with young people are very helpful in this process.

Outside of praying with the Scriptures, attending Mass, and being present at Eucharistic adoration, we have to be careful not to force young people to pray a certain way all the time. It makes plenty of sense to encourage them to pray using methods and devotions that are effective for us personally, because we can teach by example and speak with clarity and passion about those methods. However, it is good to respect the fact that not everyone is inspired by the same forms of prayer. There is great power in learning to grow into certain kinds of prayer. And this is something to discern and discuss with the pastor, other adults involved with the ministry, and even the young people themselves.

It requires humility and effort to provide young people with valid experiences of different devotions in order to help them find ways to pray that are effective for them at this stage in their lives. This can include but is not limited to praying the Angelus, the holy Rosary, the Chaplet of Divine Mercy, proven formal prayers such as the peace prayer of St. Francis of Assisi and the "Take Lord, receive" prayer of St. Ignatius of Loyola, charismatic prayer of praise, and a wide variety of novena prayers and prayers for the intercession of the saints. A range of prayer experiences can help youth learn to pray now and prepare them for the future as their prayer life develops and changes over time.

> *"Remember that good confessions and good Communions are the first steps to a sound education."*
> —St. John Bosco

4. LIVING IN THE TRUTH

Handing on the faith to others, especially young people, is different than handing on the truths of grammar, biology, or economics. Essential information about the arts and sciences can be passed along in a formal setting, like that of a classroom, by a teacher who is trained and knowledgeable. This teacher may not inspire passion, further inquiry, or a desire to pursue a profession in that field, but essential information for a basic understanding and the capacity to pass exams can be transferred.

Handing on our Christian faith is a very different story. It involves not just the exchange of information that can be memorized or quickly typed into a PC or tablet, but an invitation to enter a relationship with the living God. This process is quite delicate and demanding; it is an invitation both to get to know facts about almighty God and to encounter him, to engage him in genuine relationship, and in the end, to surrender our whole life to him. As a consequence, this kind of formation and leadership asks much more of the formator.

The personal example of the one extending this invitation is eminently important. Their love for God needs to be obvious. It is best if they are committed and zealous about living the faith. They do not need to be perfect, but they need to be striving to grow in their love for God. It is most helpful if they are humble enough about their weaknesses so as not to be hypocritical. Some fruits of the faith need to be visible, especially joy, regular prayer, and a genuine care for young people.

The capacity to hand on the faith demands being able to build trust. This begins with care. If the young people sense that you truly care for them, they will begin to open the door of their hearts. When they begin to grasp that you are not hanging out with them out of duty, for a salary, or for personal gain, they become more willing to listen to what you have to say about topics more important than the weather and the latest version of the hottest video game. They soon are willing to hear you speak about the one who gives meaning to your life. More on the importance of care to come.

Additionally, we build trust in our relationship with the young through transparency. It is nearly impossible to get a young person to listen to you unless you are authentic and open. We help create a trusting environment when, without being selfish, we are up-front about our plans, intentions, and motivations. We turn once again to the example of Christ. His whole life was transparent; he had nothing to hide. Our Lord confirmed his commitment to this very attractive element of his life at the time of his passion during his conversation with Caiaphas and the synagogue officials: "I have spoken openly to the world; I have always taught in synagogues and in the temple, where all Jews come together; I have said nothing secretly" (John 18:20). Jesus was the truth. He spoke the truth. His life was an open book.

This transparency of Jesus' life, coupled with his enormous patience, quickness to forgive, and passion for getting people on the path toward the Father, encouraged others' trust in him, as well as an openness and vulnerability in his disciples that helped prepare their hearts for the transforming grace of the Gospel and a brand-new, life-giving relationship with almighty God. Jesus' example of honesty, transparency, and commitment to the truth paved the way for an openness to the fullness of his message.

In contrast, when teachers or youth leaders come across like they have something to hide and are hesitant to share genuinely and appropriately who they are, they discourage a relationship of trust. When they seem as if they have a hidden agenda or portray an attitude that a student is not worthy of getting to know them, youth workers put up barriers that prevent the grace of evangelization. With that approach, young people do not want to hear what you have to say about the person of God or his marvelous deeds.

This lack of trust is a great obstacle to handing on the faith. It keeps the people you are trying to reach from opening their hearts to God. It discourages them from opening up to you, offering their deeper questions, sharing their struggles with living the faith, and admitting their fears, which can be a great barrier to growing in faith.

Consistency is one more critical characteristic of those serving young people. If we are not true to our word, we chip away at trust. If we are inconsistent in our attendance at regularly planned gatherings, if we promise to follow up with an email and don't, if we offer to show up to a sporting event and skip it without prior notification, young people will quickly lose their capacity to trust us. This in turn damages their capacity to embrace what we are saying about God. However, when we are true to our word in everyday interactions with them, they are more inclined to listen when we share about our love for God and even to accept a challenge to step up their prayer or avoid certain sinful behaviors.

5. BUILDING HEALTHY RELATIONSHIPS

Jesus was a master evangelizer because he was a master builder of relationships. He reached out and actively approached people in all sorts of places, including the local well, the tax collector's office, the synagogue, the road to Emmaus, and the house of a Pharisee. He engaged them in conversation and found out what was important to them: "Go get your husband"; "What were you discussing along the way?"; "What do you want from me?" He extended a deep sense of care by forgiving them, healing them, feeding them, and forming their minds and hearts. He called them to join him: "Come follow me"; "Come after me and I will make you fishers of men." He sent them to share in his own precious ministry: "As the Father has sent me, even so I send you . . ." (John 20:21).

We need to take our lead from Jesus and learn the art of building healthy, selfless, Christ-centered relationships with young people. It consistently proves to be most important for the process of evangelization of the young Church. The Second Vatican Council spoke of this need: "Adults should be anxious to enter into friendly dialogue with the young, where, despite the difference in age, they could get to know one another and share with one another their own personal riches" (*Apostolicam Actuositatem*, 12).

When building relationships with others, including the young, occasionally sharing our own personal riches assists the process. Young people enjoy hearing about our personal interests, an occasional story about our family, a prudent example of a bump along the way on our journey of faith, or a powerful moment of prayer in our lives. These stories make us real, remind them of our humanity, and help build friendly relationships.

At the same time, there is also a great need for prudence on this front. We must always make sure that our interactions and conversations are fully committed to assisting young people on their journey of faith. We should never share something personal with a young person for our own gain. We must not use these youth in our ministry in any way to meet our individual needs, as a sounding board, as a place of advice for our personal lives, or as an opportunity to vent frustrations. On the contrary, we need to be far enough along on our own journey to emotional health and maturity to remain focused on the young people, their needs, and the goal of helping them draw close to Christ.

The community has an important role in the accompaniment of young people; it should feel collectively responsible for accepting, encouraging and challenging them. All should regard young people with understanding, appreciation and affection, and avoid constantly judging them or demanding of them a perfection beyond their years."
—Pope Francis, *Christus vivit*, 243

A RESPONSE IN CARE

The most defining element of Jesus' encounters with individuals in the Gospels is that they walk away with the conviction that he deeply cares for them personally. Since the love he offers is genuine and divine, this encounter is overwhelming and completely changes their lives forever. Love is the greatest gift Jesus gives to his followers. His deep care is manifested in a variety of ways; it is tailored to the individual and their greatest needs in the moment. According to his wisdom and love, it might be a word of forgiveness, the healing touch of his hand, the penetrating glance that pierces the soul and reveals his infinite love, or the unexpected offer to come follow him. Regardless of the specifics of the situation, the Gospels are full of momentous encounters that change lives through the power of God's loving care.

Devotees of St. John Bosco usually argue that the most unique element of his enormously effective educational method, the Preventive System, is the pillar of Loving Kindness (the other two pillars are Reason and Religion). He built his method around the concept of extending to young people the love God has showered upon us. Don Bosco was convinced that the greatest motivator of the human being is love. By loving young people and teaching them to love God, you can motivate them to live for him and attain the highest spiritual and moral goals. He spoke often of the art of winning the hearts of young people.

Let's ponder some critical elements of the Preventive System that demonstrate the commitment to extend genuine care to God's little ones.

ACTIVE OUTREACH. St. John Bosco did not wait for young people to walk through the doors of his oratory in order to engage them and gradually bring them to Christ. To the contrary, his deep care for young people coupled with his intense faith in the Lord drove him out into the world in search of them. Like Christ the Good Shepherd, who left the ninety-nine to go in search of the one, St. John Bosco never stopped going into the piazzas where they were playing games, the factories where they were being poorly treated as child laborers, and the soccer fields where they were enjoying some exercise. Don Bosco went where he knew they were in order to meet, engage, and befriend them.

Given the culture of our day, which lends to less and less participation in the Church by too many families, the Church needs to embrace with renewed fervor this active element of evangelization. Our ministries need to be filled with an impulse to reach out and actively touch the lives of young people with the sacrificial love of Jesus. We have to fight the strong temptation to hang out in the comfort of our office, enjoying a peaceful lunch every day and waiting for the most active students to stop by for a relaxed visit. Jesus and the great saints, Francis of Assisi, Ignatius of Loyola, and John Bosco, were driven by the Holy Spirit to hit the road in search of souls for Christ. "Go, therefore, make disciples of all nations."

This commitment to an active outreach will likely demand a paradigm shift in the focus of our programs. In turn, it will also require new ways of organizing our ministry so that we are able to recruit and train teams of students, volunteers, and staff who are able to actively evangelize young people.

ATMOSPHERE. This was most important to St. John Bosco. He operated with the conviction that the proper education of young people takes place in an atmosphere that is cheerful, friendly, and full of genuine care. He worked hard to create a family spirit, an environment where the Salesians would not act like authoritarians, but rather like caring fathers. An element of this genuine care is a real, consistent focus on the welfare of the student. When they notice that you regularly focus on their well-being, ask thoughtful questions about their lives, follow up at a later time with relevant questions based upon previous conversations, and spend little time speaking about yourself, they begin to grasp that you are really present to them for their sake. St. John Bosco remarked, "You will obtain anything from your children if they realize that you are seeking their own good."

AVAILABILITY. Another mark of St. John Bosco's style of education is simply being available, especially outside of the more formal settings of the classroom, workshop, or chapel. The Salesians were to remain present to the young people throughout the day, at practically every moment that they were in their care. This means being actively present to young people in between classes, before Mass, after practice, and especially during recreation periods. It is in these "off" moments that you are able to imitate

Jesus, draw near to the students, and engage in their lives. This is when you get to really know young people, find out what is going on in their lives, find them asking much deeper questions, build relationships with them, and share some of your personal riches with them. Through this availability, this active presence outside the formal settings, young people learn of our care and become open to and curious about what motivates us, opening the door to conversations about Jesus Christ and the beauty of our faith in him. This availability also enables us to be present to their interactions with other students, aware of potential problems that are developing, and able to defuse them or address them before they become more serious. This is a fundamental aspect of the Preventive System of St. John Bosco.

COUNSELING. This describes the Salesians' efforts to correct poor behaviors and encourage new, better behaviors. Public corrections should be avoided at all cost, because most young people end up being more focused on and influenced by the fact that they were embarrassed in front of their peers than by the intention and purpose of the correction. When needed, such counseling moments should take place in private and with as little publicity as possible. They should be kept short, informal, and free from scolding and nagging. A brief "whispering in the ear" is always more effective than a public scolding. When we know a kid well from exercising this relational ministry, we can keep the "counseling" short and to the point.

PREVENTION. As the name implies, a very significant practical application of Don Bosco's Preventive System is prevention. Don Bosco was profoundly influenced by his experience as a young priest serving at a juvenile jail. He was so moved with pity for these young boys whose hearts were already hardened and whose lives were bruised and damaged that he committed himself wholeheartedly to preventing the kinds of actions and attitudes that lead young people down the road to jail. On a more theoretical level, he was committed to putting the good before them in such positive and encouraging ways that they would be inclined to choose the good and forsake selfish and harmful paths.

Practically speaking, St. John Bosco taught his confreres to be truly available to the students, which includes being aware of tensions developing among kids out on the playground, which ones are having a bad day, what the negative tendencies are among the more troubled students, whose families are crumbling and leaving their children extra vulnerable at the moment, etc. Availability coupled with attentiveness makes it possible to cut off difficulties at the pass, to prevent real problems before they begin. So, for example, a trained youth worker engaged with a group of students may notice that one student is having problems at home, slowly developing anger issues, and today getting rather upset on the soccer field. One strategy would be to pull this student aside, get a quick drink of water with him, ask him how his day is going, and then ask him to run a really important errand for you. This gets the kid out of a frustrating situation before it explodes, reminds him of your care, and distracts him with a needed task. The Latin word at the origin of this principle of prevention is *praevenire*, which can be translated as "to foresee" or "to provide." There is an art to foreseeing and preventing difficulties and providing for students so as to give them positive alternatives to the many challenging and harmful choices that come up in life.

CONTROL YOUR ANGER. This is the final Salesian principle for our present discussion. St. John Bosco demanded that his brothers understand how damaging angry outbursts can be for the proper education of young people. Young people do not react well to anger. It takes the focus off the present activity or lesson and puts it on the teacher or youth worker. It ruins the authority of the teacher or leader in much the way hypocrisy does. They become saddened and frustrated that the teacher or youth worker can't control their anger and they lose respect and that all-important trust. Sometimes it leads to a kind of game to get the teacher angry again; it turns into a way to try to manipulate or control the teacher and keep them from doing what they are supposed to be doing. On this topic, Don Bosco turned to his patron saint, St. Francis de Sales, who said, "I am afraid to lose in a quarter of an hour that little sweetness that I have gathered up, drop by drop, like dew, in the vessel of my heart through the efforts of twenty years."

The saint from Turin wanted all those who worked with him and his kids—the Salesians, the Daughters of Mary, Help of Christians, and his Salesian Cooperators—to be developing a level of affective maturity and a life of virtue that enables them to exercise enormous control over their emotions, particularly their anger. Don Bosco was fond of saying to those he trained, "We must not allow the shadow of anger to darken our countenance"; "Self-control must rule our whole being—our mind, our heart, our lips"; and "Let nothing disturb you." So, quite simply, there is no place for anger in the Preventive Method.

"Be angry but do not sin; do not let the sun go down on your anger . . . Let all bitterness and wrath and anger and clamor and slander be put away from you, with all malice."
(Ephesians 4:26, 31)

"There is also a special need to accompany young men and women showing leadership potential, so that they can receive training and the necessary qualifications."
—Pope Francis, *Christus vivit*, 245

DEVELOPING GIFTS AND LEADERSHIP SKILLS

An additional quality in those who serve the young that flows from this genuine care is the ability to help them discover and develop the gifts and talents God has given them for the increase of their self-worth and for the building up of God's kingdom. Sometimes the students are at least vaguely aware of these gifts and simply need some friendly encouragement. Often, they have no awareness of certain God-given gifts and talents. They are very pleasantly surprised when we point them out and confidently encourage their use.

I am referring here to a wide range of talents that God can bestow on a young person. A few obvious ones include organization, athletics, teaching the faith, leading prayer, leadership, liturgical music, having a heart for service, joyfulness, and humor. There is an art to this process, which means this skill can be developed. It requires caring enough to perceive these gifts and find ways for them to develop the talents God has given them.

We can be a further blessing to these students by providing, either in our ministry or in another setting, a practical context for the exercise and development of those gifts. Taking the additional time to actually help them develop the skills that we discover demands even more from us.

Effective evangelization and education of young people demands the kind of care that flows from a sacrificial love for them. This sacrificial love flows from the cross of Christ, the tree of life, taking root in the depths of our hearts, gradually transforming us and ultimately spilling over into our service of God's little ones. Our service becomes the process of allowing Christ's light to shine through us.

A RESPONSE IN FREEDOM

1. GOD'S GREAT GIFT TO HUMANITY

Human freedom is one of the great wonders of the world. When God fashioned us in his image and likeness, he bestowed upon us extraordinary powers and capacities. His explosive love drove him to share with us the capacity to know, love, and will, which together enable us to make decisions in freedom. This combination of gifts grants to man a tremendous dignity. It also grants a power that is almost incomprehensible. We can think, reason, choose, and love. In addition, God gave us the world to cultivate and exercise dominion over. As a result of all these gifts, we have the capacity to achieve great good or great destruction.

Put simply, God makes us free that we might love him. His love is so rich, so deep, so intense, and so life-oriented that he fashions every human being with the gift of freedom so that we might turn around and give ourselves freely back to him, radically, completely, as a generous response to his love.

One of the seminal documents of Vatican II, *Gaudium et spes*, addresses God's gift of freedom and states that he "willed that man should be left in the hand of his own counsel so that he might of his own accord seek his creator and freely attain his full and blessed perfection by cleaving to him" (*Gaudium et spes*, 17).

This original purpose of creating men and women remains so important to God that he refuses to take away our human freedom, even though we so easily abuse it, sometimes in the most horrific ways. How can we not cringe when we ponder what we, as human beings, have done with our freedom—abortion, ethnic cleansing, world wars, atomic bombs, sexual abuse of children, atheism, etc.? Yet human freedom is so critical to our response in love to God that he continues to respect it even though we often use it in selfish and destructive ways.

2. SIN ABUSES AND DESTROYS OUR FREEDOM

Sin is the misuse of all these tremendous gifts of God. It is the use of our human freedom to say no to God, directly or indirectly. When I sin, in essence, I say to God, "I know better than you what brings me to happiness and human flourishing. I choose to do it my way, not your way. I chose to love myself more than I love you." Sin damages our relationship with God. When it is serious, or mortal, it actually cuts off that relationship. This is the greatest of all evils. Our sins also harm our relationship with our neighbor and attack our own peace of soul. It causes division in every relationship we have.

However, personal sin is more than just an abuse of our freedom. Sin, both original and personal, damages our ability to respond in freedom to God's love. Repeated sin erodes our freedom. In fact, we can actually become slaves to sin. Sin takes the focus off God and neighbor and directs it at our own belly button. We spend so much time gazing at our navel rather than at the face of God revealed to us through Jesus. This is an enormous problem!

3. JESUS SETS US FREE

God the Father had a solution to this enormous problem. "For God so loved the world that he gave his only Son, that whoever believes in him should not perish but have eternal life. For God sent the Son into the world, not to condemn the world, but that the world might be saved through him" (John 3:16–17). The Father's solution to the horrendous sins of mankind was to send his beloved Son to suffer and die for us—to take our place on the cross and grant us new life.

Christ is our hope. In him our relationship with God is restored. We are forgiven; we are healed; we are given a brand-new heart. We are set free again through the grace of the Holy Spirit, which flows from the Father and the Son. "But thanks be to God, that you who were once slaves of sin have become obedient from the heart to the standard of teaching to which you were committed" (Romans 6:17). How can we properly respond to this gift?

No matter what we have done, no matter how ugly our sins,

no matter how badly we have abused the gift of freedom, we have a place to turn in our pain and sorrow, a person in whom we can take refuge. "If you continue in my word, you are truly my disciples, and you will know the truth, and the truth will set you free" (John 8:31b –32).

The truth of our existence is this: We can be free only if we remain close to Jesus. We must truly become his disciples, beseech his mercy, be healed by his love, be formed at his feet by the truths of the Gospel, and respond with great generosity by handing on these gifts to the world, starting with God's little ones.

This is true because love cannot be separated from truth. Love and truth have their origin in God, and God is one. Our culture exhausts itself trying to separate the two, but it is impossible. Consequently, countless people live without either. This, in fact, is not living at all; it is dying. Without a commitment to loving others like Christ in the truth, we die slowly and painfully, with an existence marked by selfishness, depression, and anger. "The truth will set you free."

> "For freedom Christ has set us free; stand fast therefore,
> and do not submit again to a yoke of slavery. . . .
> For you were called to freedom, brethren; only do not
> use your freedom as an opportunity for the flesh,
> but through love be servants of one another."
> (Galatians 5:1, 13)

ST. FRANCIS AND FREEDOM

Faith, hope, and love bring us to a point where we want to live not for ourselves but for Christ. We choose in freedom to live completely for God. St. Francis of Assisi is a towering example of living completely for God. Let's pause and take a look at one moment in his life.

St. Francis came to know and love God so deeply that he developed an enormous freedom that was directed at the love of God and the service of his neighbor. At one point in his faith journey, he was praying before the crucifix, and in freedom, he offered this prayer to God: "O Lord Jesus Christ, two favors I beg of thee before I die. The first is, that I may, as far as it is possible, feel in my soul and in my body the suffering which thou, O gentle Jesus, sustained in thy bitter passion. And the second favor is, that I, as far as it is possible, may receive into my heart that excessive charity by which thou, the Son of God, wast inflamed, and which actuated thee willingly to suffer so much for us sinners" (Johannes Jorgensen, *St. Francis of Assisi*, 247).

Francis asked God for two incredible favors. First, he desired to feel in his soul and his body the suffering Jesus felt during his passion. What an amazing, scary request! Yet he was truly free to love, and love does such things. If it can't take the suffering away, love desires to share in the sufferings of the beloved.

Second, Francis asked to receive into his heart the charity that inflamed the heart of Jesus as he suffered for us. Francis knew there was a supernatural, infinite dimension to the love of God poured out from the cross, and he longed to dive ever deeper into it. He wanted, as much as humanly possible, to enter more fully into that divine love.

God granted his request. In that moment of prayer, Francis received a taste of the love that led Jesus to embrace the cross and the suffering he endured while nailed to it. God granted to Francis that day the extraordinary grace of the stigmata, the visible, physical manifestation of the five wounds Jesus received on the cross. Francis lived with those five open wounds for the rest of his earthly life. His acceptance of this grace remains a permanent reminder of the heights to which we can use our human freedom to respond to the love and truth of God.

CONCLUSION

A committed life of prayer opens our hearts to God's infinite grace: "where sin increased, grace abounded all the more" (Romans 5:20). The Holy Spirit is given the opportunity to grab hold of our hearts and set them on fire for God. Sacrificial love, deep faith in Jesus, endless hope, and heroic virtue become desirable and real. Jesus said to his disciples, "Truly, truly, I say to you, he who believes in me will do the works that I do; and greater works than these will he do, because I go to the Father" (John 14:12).

> *"Then Jesus told his disciples, 'If any man would come after me, let him deny himself and take up his cross and follow me.'"*
> (Matthew 16:24)

CONCLUSION

How can I not express a profound gratitude to almighty God for his active pursuit of me? How many times has he left the ninety-nine to search me out? How often has he noticed that I was worn out and dejected and then drawn near to engage me, bring me his comfort, and set my heart on fire? How many times has the Lord sent a mentor, a passage from Scripture, or a marvelous piece of religious art to help me keep my eyes fixed on Jesus and rekindle my love for him? Of course, I must proclaim that the Lord has remained so humbly yet powerfully present to me through his real presence in the tabernacle, before which I have spent a holy hour nearly every day of my life since the seminary.

Lord Jesus, you have been my rock, my Savior, and my most faithful friend. Your presence, your mercy, and your love have transformed me and impelled me to share this priceless treasure with the world as your priest servant. I can say with St. Paul, "For this I toil, striving with all the energy which he mightily inspires within me." Lord Jesus, I can't possibly thank you enough for the countless times you have chosen to draw near and reveal to me that you delight in me!

It is hard to bring this work to a conclusion without pausing and thanking those readers who are dedicated to bringing the light and love of Christ into the lives of young people. The truth is that our youth need more than ever faith-filled, emotionally healthy, joyful adults who are willing to spend boatloads of time building relationships, earning trust, truly caring for them, and slowly inviting them to be transformed by the light and love of Christ and, ultimately, to become evangelizers of their peers. I praise God for your willingness to strive to be one of those great gifts to the Church and for your support of others who are on the same path. You are a breath of fresh air at a difficult moment in the Church's history.

A word of thanks needs to be sent up to God for all the young people with whom I have been privileged to journey through the years. You have been a sacrament to me, just like the poor, of God's presence in my life. Jesus is so present in you, even when you can't see it, that to welcome you is to welcome Christ and to welcome the Father as well. You have been a cause of immeasurable joy in my life. Some of the greatest moments I've experienced have been when one of you truly discovers in the depths of your being the personal love of God, grasps the immense beauty of the Eucharist, develops the habit of daily prayer, discovers a new gift while serving your neighbor in need, makes the agonizing decision to turn from a sinful habit or relationship, or decides to become a youth worker. You are priceless!

So, turning again to the youth workers, I invite you as charitably and as firmly as I might to increase your commitment and heartfelt devotion to a life of deep, daily prayer. The Church needs effective youth workers, and we can't love God authentically without a life of focused prayer. Nor can we help young people encounter Christ without loving him and knowing him well ourselves. We can't gather a group of effective youth workers around us if we are not leading by the example of our own lives.

People, especially the young, know whether our lives are rooted in Christ through prayer—by the way we pray in public settings, speak lovingly about Jesus in everyday discourse, conduct ourselves in the midst of complicated circumstances, and care for them personally.

If you have not developed the habit of daily prayer, get started. Take baby steps and begin with one simple form of prayer that you will practice each day. Once you do that for a month or so, consider adding another form of prayer, perhaps at a different time of the day. Consider getting a mentor, accountability partner, or spiritual director to assist you in this process.

If you pray regularly, ask the Lord to set on your heart a new, additional way to spend time with him, which will enrich your relationship with him at this moment in your life. Perhaps the Lord will ask you to go more regularly to daily Mass, pray with the readings given by the Church for Mass each day, build your devotion to Mary with the Angelus or the Rosary, explore a new devotion such as the Chaplet of Divine Mercy, or start to examine your conscience at the end of the day.

If your prayer life is strong and more advanced, ask the Lord for the grace to keep pressing forward. In the book of Hebrews, we are challenged, "Strive for peace with all men, and for the holiness without which no one will see the Lord" (Hebrews 12:14). It might mean for you the addition of a new form of prayer or an extra time for prayer in your day. It might mean reinvesting in the practices you have already developed and making sure that your heart is truly present to the Lord during those regular times. Again, a good spiritual director can be quite helpful at this stage of the journey as well.

Attitude is always important. Do I struggle each day to fit God into my busy life, or do I build my life around my daily commitment to him, knowing that he is Lord of my life and will help me take care of all my other responsibilities?

While a healthy, Spirit-led commitment to daily prayer demands that we put forth effort to build our relationship with God, let us never forget what we read in the very first paragraph of the *Catechism of the Catholic Church*: "God, infinitely perfect and blessed in himself, in a plan of sheer goodness freely created man to make him share in his own blessed life. For this reason, at every time and in every place, God draws close to man."

ABOUT THE AUTHOR

Father Jack Peterson, Y.A., is the Consecrated Cleric Assistant Director and the Director of Mission and Development for Youth Apostles, a Catholic community of single, married, and consecrated laymen and consecrated clerics who are dedicated to the service of young people. He entered Youth Apostles as a layman in 1981 and has held several leadership posts in the community, including serving for 12 years as the General Director.

A native of Northern Virginia, Father Jack received Holy Orders in the Diocese of Arlington in 1989. He has served as the parochial vicar at five parishes in the diocese, and has maintained a steady involvement in youth, college, and young adult ministry that began well before his priestly ordination.

Father Jack has given numerous seminars, talks and retreats to youth workers, teachers and audiences across the country on different aspects of faith, spirituality and youth ministry.